THE BOOK OF HAGGAI

THE BOOK OF HAGGAI

A Study Manual

by

RICHARD WOLFF

BAKER BOOK HOUSE
Grand Rapids, Michigan

Library of Congress Catalog Card Number: 67-18202

PHOTOLITHOPRINTED BY CUSHING - MALLOY, INC.
ANN ARBOR, MICHIGAN, UNITED STATES OF AMERICA
1967

CONTENTS

INTRODUCTION

1. HISTORICAL BACKGROUND

It was a dramatic hour in the history of Israel when Cyrus, king of Persia, conquered Babylon in 539 B.C. The fall of Babylon marked a new era in the history of the world. Cyrus laid the foundations of the largest political organization in pre-Roman antiquity.

Cyrus, the Persian, had become "king of Anshan" in 559, but as a vassal of the Medes. He plotted revolt against the Median overlord and found a natural ally in the Babylonians. Nabonidus, king of Babylon, favored the cult of the moon-god Sin at the expense of the Babylonian gods. His father

> "seems to have been the chief priest of the once famous temple of the moon-god Sin in Mesopotamian Harran. Since the last flicker of Assyrian rule had been stamped out in 610, Harran had remained in the hands of the Medes, who had permitted the temple to lie in ruins. Quite literally, it was the life-dream of Nabonidus to restore that temple, amid whose ruins his father was still living. But this required that Harran should first be taken from the Medes."[1]

Nabonidus entered into an alliance with Cyrus against the Medes. This coalition gave Cyrus the necessary backing and he rebelled against Media, rapidly conquering Ecbatana, capital of the Medes (550 B.C.).

> "Media ceased to be an independent nation and became the first satrapy, Mada. Nevertheless, the close relationship between Persians and Medes was never forgotten. Plundered Ecbatana remained a favorite royal residence. Medes were honored equally with Persians; they were employed in high office and were chosen to lead Persian armies. Foreigners spoke regularly of the Medes and Persians; when they used a single term, it was 'the Mede.'"
>
> "By his conquest of the Median Empire, Cyrus had taken over the Median claims to rule Assyria, Mesopotamia, Syria, Armenia and Cappadocia. In a large degree, these claims were in conflict with those of Babylonia."[2]

---

[1] A. T. Olmstead, *History of the Persian Empire* (Chicago, 1959), p. 36
[2] *Ibid.*, p. 37

The coalition between Babylonia and Persia came to an abrupt end and Babylonia now sought an alliance with Egypt and Lydia against Persia. Cyrus defeated Croesus, king of Lydia, in 546 and entered the city of Babylon without a struggle in 539 B.C. It is quite probable that he obtained help from the Chaldean priests whom Nabonidus had alienated by his worship of Sin. It is true that just prior to the fall of Babylon Nabonidus had brought several deities to the capital and re-established the great New Year festival honoring the god Marduk, but it was a futile attempt to regain confidence. Babylon opened its gates to Cyrus.

> "The first principle of his policy was that various peoples of his empire should be left free in their religious worships and beliefs, for he fully understood the first principle of statesmanship – that religion is stronger than the state. Instead of sacking cities and wrecking temples he showed a courteous respect for the deities of the conquered, and contributed to maintain their shrines; even the Babylonians, who had resisted him so long, warmed towards him when they found him preserving their sanctuaries and honoring their pantheon. Wherever he went in his unprecedented career he offered pious sacrifice to the local divinities."[3]

In his victory proclamation Cyrus designates himself as a favorite of Marduk, god of Babylon. For a period of three months the gods which had been brought to the capital by Nabonidus were brought back to their respective temples with all due honor. With the gods went the instruction to restore their temples. Cyrus himself wrote:

> "I returned to the sacred cities on the other side of the Tigris, the sanctuaries which have been in ruins for a long time, the images which used to live therein and established for them permanent sanctuaries. I also gathered all their former inhabitants and returned them to their former habitations. Furthermore I resettled on the command of Marduk, the great lord, all the gods of Sumer and Akkad whom Nabonidus had brought into Babylon."[4]

The gods of Susa were returned to Elam, those of Ashur to the ancient capital and the inhabitants of these cities were also collected and restored to their homes. Since the Jews did not

---

[3]Will Durant, *Our Oriental Heritage* (Simon and Schuster, 1954), p. 353

[4]In A. J. Thompson, *Archaeology and the Pre-Christian Centuries* (Grand Rapids, 1959), p. 30 and cf. Olmstead, *op.cit.*, p. 51, 57

possess divine images, it was most fitting that the utensils of the Temple which had been looted by Nebuchadnezzar should be returned to Jerusalem. With the conquest of Babylon the provinces in Syria fell automatically to the Persians. In 538 B.C. Cyrus granted the Jewish exiles the return to Zion. This was in line with his overall policy. It is not improbable that he received help in the conquest of Babylon from the conquered nations, forcibly transported into exile. He may well have discovered in the presence of such people a source of weakness to his empire and determined to restore them to their homeland.

> "Cyrus may have seen the wisdom of having a friendly state on the border of Egypt at the time he issued the decree permitting Jews to return to their homeland."[5]

Similarly Olmstead:

> "Invasion of the Nile valley would be greatly facilitated by a bridgehead across the desert in Palestine. The road into Egypt was dominated by the ruined fortress of Jerusalem. . . ."[6]

Palestine was a buffer-state. To occupy and hold this territory was strategically important. To win the Jews, Cyrus may have determined to help them in their effort of reconstruction.

> "The substantial historicity of the Edict of Cyrus (Ezra 1:2-4; 6:3-5) in 538 has been confirmed by modern archaeological discoveries, but it is wholly unnecessary to suppose that it was followed by any wide response on the part of the Jews in the *golah*."[7]

The political intelligence of Cyrus, and above all God's providential leading, induced Cyrus to proclaim the decree we know. Everywhere he endeavored to secure the good will and cooperation of subdued nations, restoring them to their respective countries and granting them freedom of religion. The edict of Cyrus in favor of the Jews was not altogether unexpected. Jeremiah had limited the captivity to seventy years, and Isaiah had predicted the coming of Cyrus (Jer. 29:10-14 and Isa. 44:28; 45:1).

The historicity of the captivity has been denied. It has been suggested that only some of the nobles were deported, whereas

---

[5]C. F. Pfeiffer, *Exile and Return* (Grand Rapids, 1962), p. 106
[6]Olmstead, *op.cit.*, p. 57
[7]W. F. Albright, *The Biblical Period from Abraham to Ezra* (New York, 1963), p. 87

the people as a whole remained in the land. Archaeological excavations are conclusive.

> "Many towns were destroyed at the beginning of the sixth century B.C. and never again occupied; still others were destroyed and reoccupied after a long period of abandonment, marked by a sharp change of stratum and by intervening indications of use for non-urban purposes. There is not a single known case where a town of Judah proper was continuously occupied throughout the exile."[8]

All the fortified towns of Judah had been razed to the ground. A few settlements in the Negeb escaped destruction, as well as cities north of the Judaean border, such as Bethel. The archaeological evidence is decisive.

Not too many Jews took advantage of the proclamation of Cyrus giving them freedom to return to their own country. The majority preferred to remain in exile. Material prosperity detained them, and spiritual indifference predominated. They were

> "well established in their new homes, as vividly illustrated by the Egyptian papyri beginning the year 495 and the Babylonian contract tablets dating from various periods. . . . the journey was dangerous and expensive, while conditions in Judah were certainly unsatisfactory."[9]

The country was desolate, and squatters from various surrounding nations had taken advantage of the absence of the Jews and occupied the Judaean countryside. The territory occupied by the returning exiles stretched perhaps no more than twenty-five miles in a straight line. The Samaritans were openly hostile.

Of the twenty-four orders of the priests, representatives of only four orders returned from the dispersion, a total of 4289. Only seventy-four Levites gave heed to the call. The total absence of Levites in response to the first call of Ezra is striking (I Chron. 24:3; Ezra 2:40 and cf. 7:13, 14 and 8:15). Those who took advantage of the decree of Cyrus were about 50,000 persons, including servants and maids (Ezra 2:64, 65). Actually even this relatively small number bears witness to the fact that many Jews believed that a glorious future awaited them which could only be realized in their own land.

---

[8]W. F. Albright, *The Archaeology of Palestine* (London, 1954), p. 141-142
[9]*Ibid.*, p. 87

It is difficult to know exactly how many people had been deported. According to the book of Kings some 10,000 captives were brought to Babylon and only the poorest people of the land remained in Judah (II Kings 24:14). Jeremiah mentions a total of 4,600 (Jer. 52:28ff). Various solutions have been suggested to reconcile these figures. Perhaps we should read the *seventeenth* year, instead of the *seventh* year (Jer. 52:28) and assume that the word *ten* has dropped out (cf. a similar situation in II Chron. 36:9). If this interpretation is correct the total number of captives would be 10,000 with Jehoiachin (II Kings 24) and 4,600 under Zedekiah (Jer. 52). It is possible that these accounts only give the number of adult persons of the male sex, which would increase the total number of exiles considerably. If *before* the first capture of Jerusalem prisoners of war had already been deported to Babylon they would naturally join the later exiles and swell their ranks. The time that elapsed between the first deportation and the return from the exile was nearly two generations. This, combined with the fact of relative prosperity and favorable living conditions easily explains how 50,000 persons could return from the exile and still only represent a minority of the total Jewish population in exile.

The first act of the new Jewish colony was to build the altar of God on its ancient foundations and to re-institute the important feasts of the seventh month (Ezra 3:2, 3). They also hired workmen, purchased material and laid the foundations of the Temple in the second year (Ezra 2:68, 69 and 3:7-13). A spirit of despondency gained the upper hand among those who had seen the first Temple in its glory. Discouragement and gloom settled over the entire nation. Finally the opposition of surrounding nations brought the entire undertaking to a complete stop. At first the Samaritans offered their help, but when it was refused they bitterly opposed the Jews (Ezra 4:1-5). They hired counselors against the Jews and intrigued at the Persian court. Cyrus had permitted and even encouraged the restoration of local deities and of religious institutions. This wide autonomy "offered a ready-made instrument of power and focus of discontent which ambitious native leaders might use to organize revolt."[10] Under the circumstances it would be easy to accuse the Jews of treason. Was not the reconstruction of the Temple connected with messianic aspirations. Messianic hopes could be twisted to imply a plot on the part of the Jews against

---

[10]William H. McNeill, *The Rise of the West* (Chicago, 1964), p. 128

the Persians. The Jews were discouraged, and the reconstruction of the Temple stopped.

Cambyses had followed Cyrus in 529 B.C. "Without doubt he seems to have been a wild despot, committing many atrocities in his drunkenness."[11] He conquered Egypt in 525, but expeditions against Nubia and Carthage failed. Persian armies frequently marched through Palestine and this could only have devastating effects on the small Jewish community. Cambyses died in 522 B.C. under obscure circumstances (probably suicide) and his death was followed by a period of general anarchy under the short reign of Smerdis who was slain by Darius. The death of Smerdis "brought renewed hopes of national independence, which bred a perfect orgy of revolts among the subject peoples."[12] That these international upheavals left their mark in Palestine is self-evident. For two years revolts broke out all over the empire and Darius fought one campaign after another.

Meanwhile, encouraged by Haggai, Zechariah and Zerubbabel, the Jews resumed the rebuilding of the Temple in the second year of Darius, 520 B.C. This came to the attention of Tattenai, governor of the province Beyond the River. Tattenai questioned their right to build the Temple: Who gave you a decree to build this house and to finish this structure? The Jews appealed to the decree of Cyrus. A search was made in the royal archives, and in Ecbatana a scroll was found vindicating the claim of the Jews (Ezra 5:1-17). Thereupon Tattenai received word from Darius that the reconstruction should proceed and that royal revenue should be used to help the builders. Everything needed by the priests for the offerings should be provided so that the priests may offer "pleasing sacrifices to the God of heaven, and pray for the life of the king and his sons" (Ezra 6). With this encouragement the undertaking was rapidly brought to completion in the sixth year of Darius, 516 B.C. (Ezra 6:15).

Tattenai is known through a document from Babylon dating from a few years later, actually 502.[13] He was responsible to Hystanes, satrap of Babylon and Beyond the River.

The attitude of Darius, reconfirming the decree of Cyrus and allowing the reconstruction of the Temple is in harmony with archaeological evidence. He promoted religion wherever he went. He honored the temple of Apollo, and "in Egypt his

---

[11]*Encyclopedia Britannica*, art. "Cambyses"
[12]Olmstead, *op.cit.*, p. 110
[13]J. A. Thompson, *op.cit.*, p. 40

name appears on the temples which he built in Memphis, Edfu and the Great Oasis."[14]

This brief historic sketch establishes clearly that the Jews could have rebuilt the Temple immediately upon returning to the homeland, i.e., immediately after 538. Yet, even when conditions improved under Darius, they waited a full year and needed to be stirred up by the prophetic voices of Haggai and Zechariah before they resumed building and completed the reconstruction (in 516). It was the objective of Haggai to arouse the people from their spiritual lethargy and indifference.

2. THE PROPHET

Very little is known about Haggai. His name is unique in the Old Testament. It means *festal* or *festive* (cf. the Roman name *Festus* and Gen. 46:16 and I Chron. 6:30 where we find Haggi and Haggiah). It has been conjectured that the name was given in anticipation of the joyous return from the exile. Others assume that it is indicative of the joyous character of his predictions. Perhaps Haggai was born on a feast day. The name has been discovered at Nippur on a tablet from the fifth century B.C.[15] The name frequently appears in the Elephantine papyrus, as well as in the Talmud. Outside of his own book the prophet is mentioned in Ezra 5:1 and 6:14. An indirect mention of Haggai occurs in Zechariah, who speaks of the words proclaimed to his generation "by the mouths of the prophets" *regarding the reconstruction of the Temple* (*Zech.* 8:9). In the apocryphal book of I Esdras, Haggai is named twice (6:1 and 7:3 and cf. II Esdras 1:40). A reference to the prophecy of Haggai is found in Sirach 49:11 and the Minor Prophets are mentioned in the same context (v. 10):

> "And moreover, as for the Twelve Prophets, –
> May their bones flourish in their place,
> Who recovered Jacob to health,
> And delivered him by confident hope.
> How shall we magnify Zerubbabel –
> He indeed, was a signet on the right hand. . . ."

With this last sentence compare Haggai 2:23. Aside from these direct and indirect references, we possess virtually no information regarding Haggai. According to Talmudic tradition he was

---

[14]*Encyclopedia Britannica,* art. "Darius"
[15]Hilprecht, *Palestine Exploration Fund Quarterly,* Jan. 1898

a member of "the Great Synagogue," a group of leaders of church and state. A misinterpretation of 1:13 had led some to think that Haggai was an angelic messenger in human form. Already Jerome refuted this bizarre exegesis. According to one tradition Haggai prophesied in exile of the return, whereas others state that he returned to Judea in his youth, survived the completion of the Temple and was buried near the sepulchres of the priests.[16] All these traditions are devoid of historic value. Ewald inferred from Haggai 2:3 that the prophet belonged to the small number who had seen the first Temple.[17] If so, he delivered these prophecies when he was about eighty years old.

Jewish tradition affirms that the three post-exilic prophets died within one month, namely upon the completion of the Temple. The reason for this strange thought was that the "spirit of prophecy" departed from Israel when the second Temple was completed. Another curious tradition relates that Haggai was the author of several ceremonial regulations and that, together with Zechariah and Malachi, he "introduced into the [Hebrew] alphabet the terminal forms of the five elongated letters."[18]

The Vulgate attributes Psalm 111 to Haggai; the Peshitta, Psalm 125 and 126; the Septuagint, Psalm 137. The Septuagint and the Peshitta, Psalm 146, 147 and 148. Finally, in all three versions Psalm 145 is assigned to Haggai. Perhaps some of these psalms were introduced into the Temple service upon the recommendation of Haggai and Zechariah.[19]

3. THE PURPOSE OF THE PROPHET

Haggai had to contend against unconcern, torpor, despondency and unbelief. To rouse the people from their indifference, from spiritual apathy and moral insensibility, was the task of Haggai.

Years had elapsed since the first attempt to rebuild the Temple. During all this time the Jews eagerly reconstructed their own homes and found time to beautify their own dwellings (1:4). No doubt many excuses were presented. Perhaps some influential Jews claimed that

---

[16]See *Jewish Encyclopedia,* art. "Haggai," for additional details

[17]Ewald, *Propheten des Alten Bundes* (Göttingen, 1868), p. 178

[18]G. A. Smith, *The Book of the Twelve Prophets* (New York, 1898), p. 232. The author mentions several other traditions and indicates their sources.

[19]For detailed information regarding the Jewish and Christian traditions regarding Haggai see T. André, *Le Prophète Aggée* (Paris 1895), p. 10 ff.

"as the prophecy of the seventy years applied to the Temple as well as to the capivity in Babylonian, and [since] they were only yet in the sixty-eighth year, the proper time for rebuilding the Temple had not arrived."[20]

It is indeed remarkable, that

"just as there were seventy years from the first occupation of Jerusalem by the Chaldees to the first year of Cyrus, so there were exactly seventy years from the destruction of the Temple to the edict of Cyrus."[21]

Perhaps such a "theological" reason was adduced to excuse their negligence. On the other hand, could it not be said that their condition contrasted advantageously with the situation of those who had stayed behind in the land of exile? Had they not returned to Judea? Had they not erected an altar and recognized their indebtedness to God? Had the ritual not been restored? Was this not sufficient? Had they not subsisted many years in Babylon without Temple, altar and sacrifice? There were other alleviating circumstances. Harvest calamities plagued the small community (1:6, 9-11 and 2:15 and 19). Their economic condition was certainly not improved by the armies of Cambyses marching through Palestine on their way to Egypt. The reconstruction was not politically prudent in view of the opposition of the Samaritans. Perhaps there were internal dissensions in the small colony (Zech. 8:10).

At this critical moment in the history of the Jewish nation, Haggai emerged to proclaim the message of God: Be strong and work. His message could be summarized in the words of Christ: "Seek ye first the kingdom." Notice also Ephesians 2: 20-22 and the responsibility of all believers to build the temple, i.e., the church of God.

Haggai has been accused of "one-sided levitism" because of his insistence on the reconstruction of the Temple. It has been said that he was legalistic, only preoccupied with ceremonial details or ritualistic formulas. Actually the Temple was not merely an ecclesiastical building, but a "shrine within which was kept inviolate the faith of the Old Testament."[22] The building of

---

[20]E. Henderson, *The Book of the Twelve Minor Prophets* (Andover, 1868), p. 340

[21]E. Hengstenberg, *History of the Kingdom of God under the Old Testament* II (Edinburg, 1872), p. 300

[22]R. Calkins, *The Modern Message of the Minor Prophets* (New York, 1947), in loco

the Temple was the necessary expression of the faith of the post-exilic community, thus indicating that their vocation was the service of God. Besides, the rebuilding of God's House was the outward condition of God's dwelling in their midst. An "existence without the Temple would have meant [humanly speaking] the extinction of the national religion."[23] Similarly G. S. Smith: "Without the Temple the continuity of Israel's religion could not be maintained."[24]

It was essentially the messianic hope that inspired the building of the second Temple. It would be the visible sign of the restored relationship between the covenant nation and their Lord. Thus, the prophet felt what the moment needed, and that is the supreme mark of the prophet. Far from a mere ritualistic interest Haggai denounced in strong terms the utter uselessness of mere ceremonial (see notes on 2:10-18).

Haggai's results were outstanding. "It is never an easy task to persuade a whole population to make pecuniary sacrifices, to postpone private interests to public interests."[25] Haggai was a man of action. The book is a clarion call to "be strong and work."

Haggai urged the reconstruction of the Temple, external symbol of the divine presence, because it was suggestive of the real glory that attends God's presence. The Temple would also be a significant bond, linking together the Jewish community around Jerusalem and the multitudes still in exile.

Haggai and the other post-exilic prophets had the same calling. The return from the exile had not been accompanied with a pillar of cloud and fire. Foes had not been miraculously defeated, crops were not abundant, circumstances seemed contrary. These conditions were hard to understand. The task of the prophet was to resolve the doubt of the community, to explain the delay in the dawning of messianic salvation and to ratify the divine promises after a preliminary fulfillment. Haggai was equal to the task.

> "It should ever be remembered that the Jewish prophets had a twofold function to perform: They were preachers of righteousness as well as predicters of future events. To reform, to correct, to restore, was no small part of their vocation and

---

[23]A. F. Kirkpatrick, *The Doctrine of the Prophets* (London, 1909), p. 421
[24]G. A. Smith, *op.cit.*, p. 237
[25]M. Dods, *The Expositor,* Third Series V (London 1887), p. 344 ff.

ministry. They had to make ready a people for the Lord, as well as to awaken and keep alive the expectation of His coming."[26]

4. DATE

Haggai was the first of the prophets of the restoration. He ministered "in the second year of Darius the king" (1:1), i.e., 520 B.C. As to the events of the particular time see "Historical Background" and commentary on 1:1.

Haggai pronounced his four discourses within four months (1:1; 2:1; 2:10 and 2:20).

5. DIVISIONS

The divisions of the book are clearly indicated by the four messages delivered by the prophet:

1:1-15
2:1-9
2:10-19
2:20-23

It is hardly necessary to summarize these messages since the entire book consists of merely thirty-eight verses.

6. STYLE

Is Haggai the first of an inferior order of prophets? It has been said that his style betrays "poverty of thought," is "tame," "without passion," "decadent," and thus adequately reflecting the depressed and humble circumstances of his day. It is true that his language is unadorned, but he writes not without rhetorical vividness. He does not rise much above simple prose, but "preachers do not speak in poetry, but set before the people their faults or their duties, in vivid, earnest language."[27] His message is concise, earnest, impressive. "His aim was a practical one and he goes directly to the point."[28] "If Haggai told it with a meager and starved style, this was also in harmony with the oc-

---

[26] T. T. Perowne, *The Books of Haggai and Zechariah,* in "Cambridge Bible for Schools and Colleges" (Cambridge, 1908), p. 21

[27] E. B. Pusey, *The Minor Prophets* (London, 1878), p. 483

[28] S. R. Driver, *An Introduction to the Literature of the Old Testament* (New York, 1910), p. 344

casion. One does not expect it otherwise when hungry men speak to each other of their duty."[29]

The prophet frequently uses interrogation to add liveliness to his discourse (1:4 and 9; 2:3, 12, 13 and 19). His favorite formula is "Consider your ways" (or lit. "set your hearts on your ways," 1:5 and 7; 2:15 and 18). He makes use of antithesis in 1:6 and rhythm is found in the same passage, as well as in 1:9, 10 and 2:6, 8, 22. Haggai likes repetition. The word *"spirit"* is found three times in 1:14 and *"take courage"* used twice in 2:4. Other favorite expressions are *"saith the LORD"* used three times in 2:4 or *"saith the LORD of hosts"* (2:9 and 23; etc.). The oft repeated *"Zerubbabel the son of Shealtiel and Joshua the son of Jehozadak, the high priest, with all the remnant of the people"* is another characteristic of his style. "In its simple and unpretentious style his little book has something peculiarly touching about it" is the judgment of Cornill.[30]

Haggai is quoted in the New Testament in Hebrews 12:26, 27.

7. AUTHENTICITY

"Haggai has given us a mere outline of his addresses."[31] The prophecy is "the substance of his spoken utterances and no doubt written shortly after the discourses had been delivered."[32] The book is "the embodiment of many like words."[33] In this respect most commentators seem to agree. Bleek declares that the book is "without doubt both composed and issued in its present shape by the prophet whose name it bears."[34] Actually, "this book is so brief that it seems almost ridiculous to suspect its unity," and the same author adds, "its unity as a literary production is perfectly defensible."[35] Indeed, "there seems no reason for questioning the integrity of the book."[36] These state-

---

[29]G. A. Smith, *op.cit.*, p. 237
[30]C. H. Cornill, *The Prophets of Israel* (London, 1917), p. 151
[31]J. F. McCurdy in *Lange's Commentary* (New York, 1902), Introduction to Haggai
[32]C. F. Keil, *Manual of Historico-Critical Introduction* (Edinburgh, 1869), p. 420
[33]E. B. Pusey, *op.cit.*, p. 484
[34]F. Bleek, *An Introduction to the Old Testament* (London, 1875), p. 158 vol. II
[35]H. G. Mitchell, *The International Critical Commentary* (Edinburgh, 1912), pp. 28 and 31
[36]F. C. Eiselen, *The Minor Prophets* (New York, 1907), p. 552

ments represent the opinion of the overwhelming majority of commentators.

Even this small book has not altogether escaped criticism, and its content has been attributed to various authors. Böhme questioned 1:13 and the last discourse, i.e., 2:20-23.[37] His assumption regarding 2:20-23 was based on the fact that the word *prophet* is not mentioned after Haggai's name. Of course, the title is also missing in 2:13, 14! Böhme's main argument was that 2:21 is an unnecessary repetition of 2:6 – an assumption based on faulty exegesis. The whole theory is based on trivial points and the weakness of the argument is apparent. More recent commentators have not accepted his suggestions. André feels that 2:10-19 is an interpolation from a different author.[38] His main reasons are:

The third discourse (2:10-19) interrupts the connection, since the conclusion of 2:1-9 is found in 2:20-23.

As a matter of fact 2:20 could hardly follow 2:9 and André is compelled to assume that a final redactor added 2:10 and 2:20. Actually the last discourse (2:20-23) could not be the logical conclusion of the second (2:1-9) since the last one is addressed to Zerubbabel and the second one to the nation as a whole.

In 2:10-19 André discovers a different viewpoint, a "priestly legalism." This notion is based on "an exaggerated notion of the subtlety of the illustration used in 2:12 ff."[39]

André further discovers definite contradictions between this discourse (2:10-19) and the others. The first author presupposes a drought according to André, whereas the second author assumes a superabundance of moisture (1:10, 11 and 2:17). See comments on the relevant passages.

André stresses the contradiction regarding the date of the reconstruction of the Temple (1:15 and 2:18). See exposition of these verses.

Finally André notices thirteen variations in vocabulary between the two authors. It is hardly necessary to review these items in detail unless "it should be done for the sake of showing how little science is sometimes mixed with criticism."[40]

How the compilation of the two fragments was achieved; why they were united; why the fragment (2:10-19) was inserted

---

[37]Böhme in Z.A.*W*., 1887, p. 215 ff.
[38]André, *op.cit.*, pp. 24 ff.
[39]H. G. Mitchell, *op.cit.*., p. 29
[40]G. A. Smith, *op.cit.*, p. 230

in that particular place; how we are to explain the dates added by the final editor; when the ultimate fusion took place; and which fragment is the older one; all these questions are reviewed by André. It would be tedious to analyse his suggestions and it hardly seems necessary to refute these views which have not attracted more recent commentators.

By way of illustration, the question why the fragment (2:10-19) was inserted in that particular place, is answered by André, by pointing out that the book which began with a rebuke could only finish on a note of hope and promise (2:23). The fragment to be inserted (2:10-19) comes to a conclusion with the words "from this day on will I bless you." According to André this promise was too miserable a conclusion for the entire book. The author did not wish to add the fragment and to finish on this meager note and therefore inserted the fragment where we find it today.

G. A. Smith, after briefly reviewing the theories proposed by André, concludes that

> "it would be unreasonable to decide for a distinction of authorship . . . there is therefore no reason to disagree with the concensus of all other critics in the integrity of the book of Haggai."[41]

Transpositions (esp. that 2:15-19 should follow 1:15a), emendations, etc., will be considered in the exposition; see notes on 1:15.

---

[41]*Ibid.*

EXPOSITION

1:1. *In the second year of Darius the king, in the sixth month, in the first day of the month, came the word of the LORD by Haggai the prophet unto Zerubbabel the son of Shealtiel, governor of Judah, and to Joshua the son of Josedech, the high priest, saying,*

"Darius" reigned from 521 to 486 B.C. Accordingly *"the second year"* of his reign corresponds to the year 520 B.C. The Jews, without a king of their own, dated their events by the reign of the kings by whom they were subjugated. The very first word of prophecy after the captivity reminded them that they were not yet fully restored.

When Darius acceded to the throne the empire had to be reconquered and reorganized. Media, Parsa, the very homeland of Darius, Elam, Babylon under Nidintu-Bel who called himself Nebuchadnezzar III, Assyria, Egypt, virtually the entire empire revolted and rose up in arms against the new ruler. Darius added victory to victory and toward 520 B.C., when this prophecy was uttered, had regained control of most of the empire. In the winter of 519 he was on his way back to the west and Palestine lay on his road. He conquered Egypt and after a few months returned home, once again by way of Palestine. That these international events had significant repercussions in Palestine is obvious. Nationalist aspirations would be rekindled and the temptation was great to join the rebellion against the Persian overlord. The Persian armies marched through Palestine on their way to Egypt and this would certainly add economic hardship to the small Jewish colony. Darius built a canal, predecessor of the Suez Canal; it was 150 ft. wide and deep enough for merchantmen. It could be traversed in four days. This gigantic undertaking must also have had economic effects on the Jewish state.

It was not merely a period of great political upheaval. It was also an era of significant religious fermentation. Karl Jaspers finds the *axis* of history in the period around 500 B.C., or more broadly speaking in the era between 800 B.C. and 200 B.C. In this "axial period" three regions of the world entered eras of "spiritual creations" which have determined human history to this day. Jaspers makes reference to Confucius and Lao-tse in China, Buddha and various philosophical schools in India, Zarathustra in Iran, who taught a challenging view of the world as a struggle between good and evil, Heraclitus, Plato and Archimedes in Greece. Jaspers does not hesitate to write that

> "any people that attained no part in the Axial Period remained 'primitive,' continued to live that unhistorical life which had been going on for tens or even hundreds of thousands of years." He adds: "The fact of the threefold manifestation [i.e., in India, China and the West] of the Axial Period is in the nature of a miracle, in so far as no really adequate explanation is possible within the limits of our present knowledge."[42]

Other historians have noticed the same phenomena of a "spiritual outburst" during those centuries which came to a climax in the fifth century B.C.

It would certainly be most fitting that at that time of great political, sociological, economic and spiritual upheaval the voice of God would be heard in Judea through the prophet Haggai. See additional notes in "Historical Background."

The name *Zerubbabel* probably signifies "seed [or offspring] of Babylon," i.e., born at Babylon. It would appear that Sheshbazzar, mentioned in Ezra 1:8, 11 and 5:14, 16 is to be identified with Zerubbabel (cf. Ezra 3:2, 8 and 5:2). This identification is accepted by many scholars (van Hoonacker, Hitzig, etc.).[43] Others identify Sheshbazzar with Shenazer, son of Jeconiah (I Chron. 3:18). Sin-ab-usur ("sin protect the father") could perhaps have been the common Babylonian original for both names, i.e., for Sheshbazzar and Shenazer. It has been conjectured that Shenazer (I Chron. 3:18 *shn'tsr*) was corrupted to Sheshbazzar (*shshbtsr*).

> "The relationship between Shesh-bazzar and Zerubbabel is enigmatic. Many scholars suggest that they are different names for the same individual. In Ezra 5:14, however, Shesh-bazzar is mentioned as though he were dead ('one whose name was

---

[42]Karl Jaspers, *The Origin and Goal of History* (New Haven, 1953), Part I, Ch. 1

[43]Van Hoonacker, *Zorobabel et le second temple,* extrait du 'Muséon' (Gand, 1892), p. 49

F. Hitzig, *Die zwölf kleinen Propheten* (Leipzig, 1838), in loco

> Shesh-bazzar') although Zerubbabel was clearly alive at that time. It may be that Shesh-bazzar died soon after the return to Jerusalem and Zerubbabel became his successor."[44]

It seems preferable to retain the identity of Sheshbazzar and Zerubbabel. See additional notes on 2:21.

Zerubbabel is called the son of Shealtiel in Ezra 3:2, 8; 5:2; Nehemiah 12:1; I Chronicles 3:17; Matthew 1:12; Luke 3:27 (the A.V. has Salathiel in the last three passages) and by Haggai in 1:1, 12, 14 and 2:2, 23. However, according to I Chronicles 3:19 Zerubbabel was the son of Pedaiah, brother of Shealtiel (I Chronicles 3:17-19). Luke's genealogy states that Shealtiel was a descendent of Neri (Luke 3:27). We have therefore three different accounts:

–Zerubbabel is the son of Shealtiel (Hag. 1:1)
–Zerubbabel is the son of Pedaiah, brother of Shealtiel and the grandson of Assir (I Chron. 3:17-19)
–Zerubbabel is the son of Shealtiel and the grandson of Neri (Luke 3:27)

In this connection it is important to recall the prophecy of Jeremiah (22:30) concerning Coniah (Jeconiah): "Thus saith the LORD, Write ye this man childless, a man shall not prosper in his days: for no man of his seed shall prosper, sitting upon the throne of David, and ruling any more in Judah." These words do not necessarily imply that Coniah (Jeconiah or Jehoiachin) shall be childless, but merely that none of his descendants shall "*sit upon the throne of David.*"

Zedekiah, son of king Jeconiah, died childless, and Assir, another son of Jeconiah, had apparently only a daughter (I Chron. 3:16). According to the mosaic law, the daughter of Assir would be the heiress and would therefore have to marry a man belonging to a family of her paternal tribe (Num. 27:8 and 36:8, 9). She married Neri, a descendant of David through Nathan. Luke does not mention Assir, a descendant of David through Solomon, but Neri, a descendant of David through Nathan, as grandfather of Zerubbabel – and this in harmony with the prediction of Jeremiah. From the union of Neri and the daughter of Assir sprang Shealtiel and those mentioned in I Chronicles 3:18. When Shealtiel in turn died childless his brother Pedaiah had the duty of levirate marriage (Deut. 25:

---

[44]Pfeiffer, *op.cit.*, p. 105

5-10) and Zerubbabel was their son. Legally Shealtiel was the son of Assir and grandson of Jehoiachin, actually the son of Neri. Zerubbabel was legally the son of Shealtiel, but actually the son of Pedaiah. Notice diagram No. I on the following page.

A simpler explanation is possible. It does not appear from Scripture if Jehoiachin (Jeconiah) was married or if he had any children. In I Chronicles 3:16 Zedekiah is called the son of Jeconiah, but a comparison with II Kings 24:15, 17 would establish that Zedekiah was actually the uncle of Jeconiah. Zedekiah is called "son" of Jeconiah because he succeeded him upon the throne. In I Chronicles 3:17 Assir is called the son of Jeconiah. However, instead of translating the Hebrew word as a proper name (AV) we should perhaps translate: "The sons of Jeconiah, *the captive*" (ASV and RSV). Jeconiah was transported into exile at a tender age (II Chron. 36:9) and remained in captivity for thirty-seven years (II Kings 25:27). If he had children (Zedekiah and/or Assir?) they died childless or were perhaps made eunuchs (Isa. 39:7). Jeconiah then adopted the seven sons of Neri, descendant of David through Nathan. Solomon's line failed and terminated with Jeconiah (in harmony with the words of Jeremiah). The promises given to Solomon had been conditional (I Kings 9:4, 5 and I Chron. 28:6, 7) and the king had certainly failed (I Kings 11:1-13). Shealtiel (adopted by Jeconiah) died childless and his brother Pedaiah performed the duty of levirate marriage. Zerubbabel was the offspring of this union. Thus

Zerubbabel was the (legal) son of Shealtiel and grandson of Jeconiah.

Zerubbabel was the (actual) son of Pedaiah and grandson of Neri.

Notice diagram No. II on the next page.

Zerubbabel is called governor of Judah or prince of Judah (Ezra 1:8). The Hebrew word translated governor (p-cht) is of foreign origin, and the exact derivation or root of the word is uncertain. In Ezra 5:3 it designates the civil and military ruler of a part of the Persian Empire. Zerubbabel was a governor of the third rank, responsible to Tattenai who in turn was under the satrap of "Babylon and Beyond the River."

"*Joshua's*" father had been deported into captivity (I Chron. 6:15) and his grandfather Seraiah was killed by the king of Babylon at Riblah (II Kings 25:18-21). Haggai makes his appeal

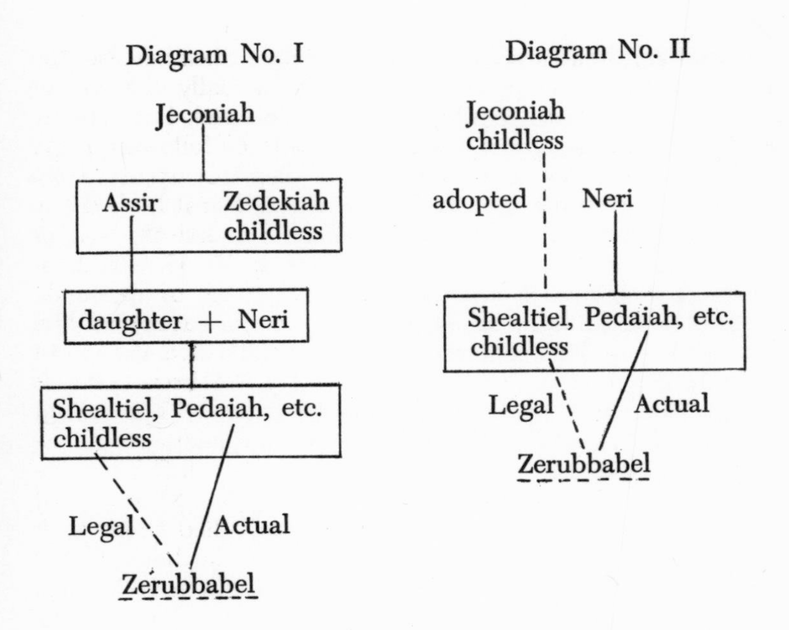

to the civil and religious leaders of his day. The completion of the task, its delay or its progress, depended on man's obedience. Zerubbabel and Joshua are addressed as representatives of the entire nation. All must build, prophet and priest, governor and people. God uses strange temple-builders. Even Darius played a significant part in God's providence in order to accomplish His goals.

Haggai spoke in the "*sixth month*" which, named according to the order of the Jewish year, was Elul (Neh. 6:15), answering to part of August and September. The prophet Zechariah began his prophetic ministry two months later (Zech. 1:1).

On the "*first day of the month*" the feast of the new moon was celebrated (Num. 10:10 and 28:11). On that day trade stopped (Amos 8:5), and the people may have taken advantage of the feast day to obtain religious instruction from the prophet (cf. II Kings 4:23). It was a suitable day where Haggai could attract the attention of the people.

> "God directs the very day to be noted . . . a precedent to us to keep in memory the days and the seasons, in which He stirs our souls to build more diligently His spiritual temple in our souls."[45]

---

[45]Pusey, *op.cit.,* in loco

Concerning the expression "*the word of the LORD*" see "Style." There is a marked difference in the usage of LORD (*Yahweh*) and God (*Elohim*). Yahweh describes the God of revelation; therefore, with but few exceptions we read of the "*word* of the *LORD*," "thus *sayest* the *LORD*," "the *commandment* of the *LORD*," etc. Anthropomorphisms are almost invariably applied to Yahweh: "*hand* of the LORD," "*voice* of the LORD," "*eyes* of the LORD," "*mouth* of the LORD" (always). The word God (*Elohim*) designates God as Creator. When David celebrates the glory of creation he speaks of God (*Elohim*), but when He refers to the God of revelation he uses LORD (*Yahweh* – Ps. 19:1, 7).

The words "*by Haggai*" should literally be translated "by the hand of Haggai." As to Haggai see the "Introduction" and on the word *prophet* see notes on 1:3.

> "If we compare our church with the Temple of the Jews, we see that in some places the foundation is not yet laid, in some the walls not built, finally that the roof yet wanteth to the perfection of the work."[46]

Rainolds compares the foundation to the planting of the church, the establishing of its walls to the teaching of the church, and the roof to church discipline, because the roof keeps those within "from annoyance of raine and weather, of heat and blasts," i.e., from sin and offenses.

Compare Ephesians 2:20-22. The fullness of the Gentiles must come in – the holy Temple, i.e., the church must be completed by the proclamation of the gospel to the end of the earth.

1:2. "*Thus speaketh the LORD of hosts, saying, This people say, The time is not come, the time that the LORD'S house should be built.*"

On the expression "*LORD of hosts*" see expository notes on 1:7.

The words "*this people*" rather than "my people" express God's displeasure.

The literal translation of the latter part of the text would be: "*Is it not time to come, time for the LORD'S house to be built?*" "To come" is an infinitive, written defectively in Hebrew, as also in Exod. 2:18; Lev. 14:48; Num. 32:9; I Kings 14:28 and Isa. 20:1; primitively the infinitive was not written differently according to Nowack.[47]

---

[46]John Rainolds, *The Prophecy of Haggai* (Edinburgh, 1864), in loco
[47]Nowack, *Handkommentar zum A.T.*, in loco

The people presented numerous excuses not to build the Temple: We have not yet sufficiently recovered from the exile; the altar has been built and is adequate in times of economic depression; it is not yet the appointed time, because seventy years have not yet elapsed since the destruction of the Solomonic Temple; it is preferable to delay the construction in order to possess the necessary means to erect a glorious structure, etc. See "The Purpose of the Prophet." As Matthew Henry pointed out, "it is bad enough to neglect our duty, but it is worse to vouch Providence for the patronizing of our neglect" (in loco). Similarly Calvin: To him who willeth to do right, the time is always present. Men are very ingenious when they wish to hide their delinquencies."[48] When did men ever say: It is not time to look after my own interests; it is not time to make money? Love of ease, greed of gain and selfishness were hidden under the mask of duty. To feed their bodies men starve their souls and forget that man does not live by bread alone. The people were orthodox, but the supreme things were relegated to a subsidiary position (cf. Matt. 23:23). Legalistic in non-essentials and lawless in weightier matters, the people deserved the rebuke of Haggai. They intended to rebuild the Temple, but – not yet.

Jesus Christ is building His church (Matt. 16:18) and Christians, as living stones are built up "a spiritual house" (I Peter 2:5), "built upon the foundation of the apostles and the prophets, Jesus Christ himself being the chief cornerstone, in whom all the building fitly framed together groweth unto a holy temple in the Lord" (Eph. 2:20, 21). The building must be completed. If the building of the Jewish Temple was so important in God's eyes, is the same not true regarding the erection of the spiritual temple of God? The rebuilding of the Temple was a necessary preparation for the first coming of Christ; the completion of the spiritual temple is a necessary preparation for the second coming of Christ (Rom. 11:25).

> "Rome [as they say] was not built in a day: No mervaile then if Jerusalem be not; for it is easier and sooner done to build the Temple of Babylon, than the Temple of Sion."[49]

Builders of the spiritual temple must expect opposition, but "build the house, and I will take pleasure in it, and will be glori-

---

[48]John Calvin, *Commentaries on the Twelve Minor Prophets IV* (Grand Rapids, 1950), in loco

[49]Rainolds, *op.cit.*, in loco

fied saith the LORD" (Hag. 1:8, 13). Men and women hewn out of the quarry of this world must be quickened by the Spirit of God, and incorporated into God's living temple.

1:3. *"Then came the word of the LORD by Haggai the prophet, saying,"*

"Then," literally "and," i.e., "therefore," or "then," God revealed His will. Cf. notes on 1:1.

"Haggai the prophet" (1:1, 3, 12 and 2:1, 10) is the LORD'S messenger (1:13), revealing God's will. In Exodus 7:1 God says to Moses: "I have made thee [constituted thee] a god to Pharaoh: and Aaron thy brother shall be thy prophet." Aaron is to be the mouthpiece of Moses. The same concept is found in Exodus 4:16: "And he [i.e., Aaron] shall be thy [Moses'] spokesman unto the people: and he shall be, even he shall be to thee instead of a mouth." The ordinary Hebrew word for prophet (*nbi'*) is derived from a verb (*nb'*) which means to bubble forth, like a fountain. The word could indicate the "bubbling up" of the divine message, as waters issue from a hidden fountain (cf. Ps. 45:1 "my heart overfloweth"). The prophet was a spokesman of God. The discourse of Haggai is determined by the Holy Spirit and Haggai proclaims the divine will to the nation.

> "The two great objects of the institution of prophecy were to direct the inner life of God's people into harmony with the commands and the spirit of the law, and to point forward to Him who was to fulfill both the Law and the Prophets."[50]

The last word of this verse (*'mr*) is usually translated by "*saying*" and is used commonly in Hebrew. It means to mutter, to speak in a low voice – especially used of the voice of God, by which oracles were revealed to the prophets. Maybe it could be translated "so has Yahweh revealed" or "the voice of Yahweh is." The word "represents the mysterious nature of the inwardly perceived Divine voice."[51]

1:4. *"Is it time for you, O ye, to dwell in your ceiled houses, and this house lie waste?"*

Literally, "Is it time for you yourselves to dwell in your wainscotted houses [whilst, or] and this house lie waste?" "You yourselves" is an emphatic repetition (*lkhm 'tm*). "How is it

---

[50]McCurdy, *op.cit.*, in loco

[51]G. F. Oehler, *Theology of the Old Testament* II (Edinburgh, 1875), p. 333

that ye make a fit time, not only to build, but to dwell at ease in your own houses."[52] "You dwell in your luxuriously paneled homes and the Temple of God is in ruins."

The people argued: "We refuse to build now because of our political problems and in view of our economic misery." God answers: "Your sad state of affairs is due to your negligence and will certainly continue if you do not rebuild the Temple." The people may have felt that other tasks were more urgent, that the times were insecure, that the nation as a whole would not respond to the challenge to reconstruct the Temple because of their spiritual lethargy, that the priest themselves were unfaithful and satisfied with the status quo. Haggai meets these arguments. No other task is more urgent; even revolutions and wars should not deter the nation because all the events of life are under the control of God (1:4 and 2:6-9, 21-23); the clarion call to work is addressed to the nation as a whole and God Himself stirs up the spirit of the people (1:14); the leaders are challenged throughout, ritualism per se is condemned (2:10 ff) and God's blessing is promised (2:19).

"*Ceiled houses*" were most luxurious. Solomon had covered his residence with cedar (I Kings 7:3, 7) and was imitated by the kings of Judah who built themselves houses and ceiled them with cedar, and painted them with vermillion (Jer. 22:14). Contrast David's attitude, who deplored that "he dwelled in a house of cedar, but the ark of God dwelleth with curtains" (II Sam. 7:2). So David "sware unto the LORD, and vowed unto the mighty God of Jacob; surely I will not come into the tabernacle of my house, nor go up into my bed; I will not give sleep to mine eyes, or slumber to mine eyelids, until I find out a place for the LORD, an habitation for the mighty God of Jacob" (Ps. 132:2-5).

The text of Haggai is heart-searching when we consider the situation of God's spiritual temple, the church.

1:5. "*Now therefore thus saith the LORD of hosts: Consider your ways.*"

For the expression "*LORD of hosts*" see notes on 1:7.

"*Consider your ways,*" or literally "set your hearts upon your ways," is a favorite formula of the prophet and used no less than four times in this short book (1:5, 7 and 2:15, 18). The ex-

---

[52]Jamieson, Fausset and Brown, *A Commentary Critical and Explanatory* (New York), in loco

hortation is equivalent to: "Let us search and try our ways, and turn again to the LORD" (Lam. 3:40). Examine your heart, your past doings and your present estate. Our acts are "ways in which we go." What has resulted from giving pre-eminence to the problems of *this* life instead of the interests of the kingdom of God? What happened in the material realm? In the spiritual realm? Consider how you fared!

The heart is the organ of thought (Prov. 23:7), as well as the seat of the affections and emotions (Deut. 6:5). In the heart of man resides the spring of his intellectual and moral activity. It is the seat of moral impulses, both the discriminative and directive. "Heart" is thus equivalent to conscience (Job 27:6; I Sam. 14:7). It embraces the whole inner man. "Examine me, O LORD and prove me; Try my reins and my heart" (Ps. 26:2). The attitude reflected in this prayer is the purpose of the divine exhortation "by the hand of Haggai."

1:6. *"Ye have sown much, and bring in little; ye eat, but ye have not enough; ye drink, but ye are not filled with drink; ye clothe you, but there is none warm; and he that earneth wages earneth wages to put it into a bag with holes."*

The infinitive absolute is used to give additional emphasis and to express the idea of the verb abstracted from all considerations of person or time: It is so at all times, continually. It is an ever present evil. "Ye have sown much and [there is] a bringing in little; [there is] eating, but not to be being satisfied; [there is] a clothing [of oneself] and it was not for a warming to him; and he that earneth wages, earneth wages into a pierced bag." People were afraid to eat sufficient food for fear of exhausting the supply. Harvests were meager and supplies had to last. The small crops produced but little income and did not permit the purchase of warm clothing. Wage earners suffered because of insufficient salaries and inflation. You eat and drink, but not to the point of satisfaction. "No one is warm" – singular, to emphasize that this was true for each single person. Money disappeared as if it had been placed in a bag full of holes. Instead of escaping poverty by not building and keeping their means, "God brought it on them for not building." This living according to a false principle had brought disastrous results. "The events of life are hieroglyphics in which God records His feelings toward us, the key to which is found in the Bible.[53]

---

[53]T. V. Moore, *The Prophets of the Restoration,* in loco

The text furnishes a graphic description of the unprofitableness of a godless life. "Except the LORD built the house, they labor in vain that build it" (Ps. 127:1). A meager harvest was the lot of the community. Moses had predicted that in case of disobedience they would "carry much seed out into the field, and gather but little in" (Deut. 28:38). They were treading the winepress and suffering thirst (Job 24:11). Scarcity of food and hunger among the people were the logical results. "If ye walk contrary to me ye shall eat and not be satisfied" (Lev. 26:26).

> "Even in their use of the little that had been reaped, the blessing of God was wanting, as is not only evident from the words themselves, but placed beyond the possibility of doubt by v. 9."[54]

Cf. also Micah 6:14 and Hos. 4:10. Money vanished as if they had never possessed it. Regarding wages see Leviticus 19:13 and Deuteronomy 24:14, 15 (cf. Prov. 26:10 and Rom. 6:23). By way of contrast notice Luke 12:33: "Bags which wax not old, a treasure in heaven that faileth not." Again, "Seek ye first the kingdom and take no thought saying, What shall we eat? or What shall we drink? or Wherewithal shall we be clothed? After all these things do the Gentiles seek."

While the rich built themselves mansions (v. 4) and luxurious houses, they failed to help the poor. Their indifference toward God went hand in hand with unconcern toward the poor. Zechariah confirms this fact: "For before these days there was no hire for man, nor any hire for beasts; neither was there any peace to him that went out or came in because of the affliction [the adversary]: for I set all men every one against his neighbor" (Zech. 8:10). Ungodliness and unrighteousness go hand in hand (Rom. 1:18). The horizontal and vertical relations are inseparable, and the first and great commandment to love God should never be severed from "the second which is like unto it, to love thy neighbor as thyself." Callousness towards others is a sure sign that love to God is lacking (I John 3:14, 17; 4:7, 12, 13, 20, 21).

1:7. *"Thus saith the LORD of hosts, Consider your ways."* Cf. notes on 1:5.

Some critics omit the latter half of this verse, because "con-

---

[54]Keil, *op.cit.,* in loco

sider your ways" is not applicable except to past action or experience. This assumption cannot be maintained in view of 2:15 and 18. Others have rearranged the text and transposed verses 7 and 8 after 11. But 1:9-11 can hardly follow upon 1:6, since 1:6b has a "concluding character."[55] This transposition would leave verse 7 "meaningless and indefensible."[56] The expression "consider your ways" is reiterated for the sake of emphasis and urgency.

Horst[57] on the other hand, transposes verses 7 and 8 for no apparent reason, whereas Budde[58] feels that verse 8 should follow upon verse 4, and Sellin[59] prefers to place verse 8 after verse 11. The very disagreement among scholars indicates that no objective reason justifies such a transposition.

The expression *LORD of hosts* is never found in the Pentateuch, nor in the books of Joshua, Judges, Ezekiel or Daniel. The first occurrence is in I Samuel 1:3. The name expresses the absolute sovereignty of God. The word "hosts" refers to heavenly bodies and celestial spirits (Neh. 9:6). This designation emphasizes the uniqueness of the living God in contrast with the deification of the heavenly bodies by the heathen. God, the omnipotent ruler of the universe, bids us to "*consider your ways.*"

1:8. "*Go up to the mountain, and bring wood, and build the house; and I will take pleasure in it, and I will be glorified, saith the LORD.*"

Although the definite article is used (*the* mountain), Haggai does not refer to Mount Moriah or the Lebanon, but to the mountains in the vicinity of Jerusalem. The definite article is used generically; (cf. Neh. 8:15). Jerome assumed that the walls of the Temple were still standing since the Jews are called to provide wood only. This view cannot be maintained in the light of the texts of Ezra (Ezra 3:6, 10 and Hag. 2:18). Wood is put here for building material in general, and not to the exclusion of all other material.

"*I will take pleasure in it.*" God's pleasure is not in sacrifices

---

[55]Th. H. Robinson and F. Horst, *Handbuch zum A.T.* (Tubingen, 1954) p. 205
[56]Mitchel, *op.cit.,* in loco
[57]Robinson and Horst, *ibid.,* p. 205
[58]Budde in ZAW (1906), pp. 1-28
[59]Sellin, *Studien zur Entstehungsgeschichte der judischen Gemeinde,* II, (1901)

devoid of love (Micah 6:7), but "in them that fear him" (Ps. 147:11). The reconstruction of the Temple was a manifestation of true repentance and resulted from it. Does God take pleasure in a building?

> "We must consider the Temple not nakedly in itself, but in such sort as respecteth the use and signification of it."[60]

The Temple was used to serve God and foreshadowed Christ as well as the believer (Heb. 9 and 10; I Cor. 6:19; cf. p. . . . of the *Introduction*).

I will be glorified, i.e., by your obedience. You no longer despise my name, but give glory to God by your actions. The translation of the RSV "that I may appear in my glory" would seem to indicate that God would actually become visible, a thought not countenanced by the context. If the reflexive meaning is to be preferred, "I will show myself glorious" or "I will glorify myself" then Haggai would simply indicate that God would cause His blessing to flow upon the people. This is then to be construed as "as positive promise that God would show forth His glory."[61] If you are obedient then will I display my glory, i.e., bless the nation once again. "Therefore say thou unto them, Thus saith the LORD of hosts; Turn ye unto me, saith the LORD of hosts, and I will turn unto you saith the LORD of hosts" (Zech. 1:3; cf. Mal. 3:7 and James 4:8a).

Their previous negligence had led to the misery described in verse 6; their obedience would remove these evils. God will be glorified, i.e., He will pour out His blessings on the nation and the people will praise him.

The translation, "I will be glorified," seems preferable. It is not necessary to assume that the Hebrew word is written defectively and to supply one letter in order to render with Hitzig[62] "that I may feel myself honored." Context and grammar are in favor of the translation given above. For the entire thought see Isaiah 26:15.

Some rabbis conjectured that the fifth letter of the Hebrew alphabet was missing (*Kri 'kbdh*). Since this letter – when used as a numeral – stands for the number five, it had led the Tal-

---

[60]Rainolds, *op.cit.*, in loco
[61]Pusey, *op.cit.*, in loco
[62]Hitzig, *op.cit.*, in loco

mudists to the conclusion that the new Temple was deficient in five respects:

> In five things the first Sanctuary differed from the second: in (1) the Ark, the ark-cover (mercy seat), the Cherubim, (2) the fire, (3) the Shekinah, (4) the Holy Spirit (of prophecy) and (5) the Urim and Thummim.[63]

Sievers would like to transpose the verse after verse 11 because he feels that the command to go up to the mountain and to bring wood interrupts the argument of verses 7 and 9. Budde, on the other hand, would like to place this verse after verse 4.[64] Such subjective judgments cannot but lead to divergent conclusions.

For the erection of the new Temple God was pleased to use human instrumentality and the progress or delay of the work stood in direct proportion with the obedience or disobedience of the Jewish nation. The same holds true in regard to the building of God's spiritual temple, the church of Christ. The risen Master gave the commission to "go" and stressed it repeatedly! Christians are either building the Temple of God or breaking the carved work of the Temple with axes and hammers (Ps. 74:6 and cf. Matt. 12:30).

Although some may have waited for better times and others expected help from the friendly Persian overlord (Ezra 6:4), God commanded them to proceed without delay or discouragement. The work must be completed (cf. Luke 14:28-30 and contrast Gal. 6:9).

1:9. "*Ye looked for much, and lo, it came to little*: *and when ye brought it home, I did blow upon it. Why? saith the LORD of hosts. Because of mine house that is waste, and ye run every man to his own house.*"

They frequently inspected the growing crop and expected a good harvest, but "the seed of an homer shall yield an ephah" (Isa. 5:10), i.e., only one tenth of what was sown. When finally they had brought home what had been reaped, God did not add his blessing to it and it decayed. God did not blow it away, but "blew upon it," blasted, blighted, spoiled the harvest. Their eager anticipation had been precluded. "That 'why' strikes into

---

[63]Yoma 21b

[64]Budde, *op.cit.*, in loco

the inmost depths of conscience."[65] God's house is desolate and you run every man to his own house, center of your activity. "For all seek their own, not the things which are Jesus Christ's" (Phil. 2:21). Few can say with the Psalmist: "I will run the way of thy commandments" (119:32).

> Be not deceived; God is not mocked: for whatsoever a man soweth, that shall he also reap. For he that soweth to his flesh shall of the flesh reap corruption; but he that soweth to the spirit shall of the Spirit reap life everlasting. And let us not be weary in well doing: for in due season we shall reap, if we faint not (Gal. 6:7-9).

Human wisdom might have dictated a policy of cautious economy: wait for a plenteous harvest and then build the house of God. God indicates that the harvest is meager because of their neglect. Throughout Haggai stresses the pre-eminence of the kingdom of God!

On the expression, *"LORD of hosts,"* see notes on 1:7. It is most appropriate here. Haggai

> "inserts once more, between the question and the answer, the words 'is the saying of Jehovah of hosts', that the answer may not be mistaken for a subjective view, but laid to heart as a declaration of God who rules the world."[66]

Cf. Haggai 2:17.

1:10. *"Therefore the heaven over you is stayed from dew, and the earth is stayed from her fruit."*

"Therefore," on account of your self-centeredness, heaven and earth have withheld their blessings. *Heaven and earth* are personified as in Jeremiah 2:12. The American Standard Version renders: "Therefore *for your sake* the heavens. . . ." The local sense given by the Authorized Version (*"over you"*) is preferable. These calamities of nature were caused by the national disobedience which occasioned God's displeasure. Moses had announced long ago:

> "If thou wilt not harken unto the voice of the LORD, thy God, the heaven that is over thy head shall be brass, and the earth that is under thee shall be iron" (Deut. 28:23; cf. Lev. 26:19).

---

[65]Pusey, *op.cit.*, in loco
[66]Keil, *op.cit.*, in loco

Contrast the magnificent promise given by Hosea in 2:21 ff.

Notice that even "*dew*" is withheld (cf. also II Sam. 1:21 and I Kings 17:1). The remarkably copious dews of the summer months almost take the place of rain in Palestine. That the heavens shall "drop down dew" is a particular blessing (Deut. 33:28; cf. v. 13). Contrast God's promise in Zechariah 8:12. The Hebrew word translated "*fruit*" means increase or produce.

The Bible accentuates repeatedly the intimate connection between spirit and nature. The fall of man and the groan of creation are related and indicative of the deep solidarity existing between man and creation. Nature has been placed in such a relation to man that it has been affected by the various misfortunes of the human race caused by sin. The soul of the world is man and his fall and redemption affects the earth (cf. Rom. 8:19-23 and Deut. 28:15 ff.).

1:11. *"And I called for a drought upon the land, and upon the mountains, and upon the corn, and upon the new wine, and upon the oil, and upon that which the ground bringeth forth, and upon men, and upon cattle, and upon all the labor of the hands."*

These words still depend on the "therefore" of verse 10. "The Lord has called for a famine" (II Kings 8:1; cf. Ps. 105:16). God had called upon the nation, but as they refused to listen God called upon the inanimate creation and it obeyed. The word "*drought,*" or waste (*chrbh*) in the original, recalls 1:9 where we read "my house is waste" (*chrbh*). In the original the words imply the correspondence between sin and its punishment. God's house was waste, and by a just retribution God called for a waste, for desolation and devastation. The drought covered the land, even the mountains where dew seldom ceases. The drought also extended over the "*new wine and oil.*" The Hebrew word for wine is literally *must,* new wine (*tyrvsh*), apparently so called because in intoxicating it takes possession of the brain. According to Gesenius the Hebrew word is derived from a root that signifies "to take possession of" (*yrsh*). The word "oil" designates fresh, new oil. It was used as food, to anoint the body, for medicinal purposes as well as ritual. In 2:12 two different Hebrew words are used for oil and wine. André concluded that this difference in vocabulary indicates a difference in authorship.[67]

---

[67]André, *op.cit.,* p. 26 ff

> According to André one author uses the words *ytshr* (oil) and *tyrvsh* (new wine), whereas the other author uses *shmn* (oil) and *yyn* (wine); cf. 1:11 and 2:12. André "overlooks the fact that the former pair of names, meaning the newly pressed oil and wine, suited their connection, in which the fruits of the earth are being catalogued, 1:11, while the latter pair, meaning the finished wine and oil, equally suit their connection, in which articles of food are being catalogued, 2:12."[68]
>
> André likewise discovers a contradition between 1:10, 11 and 2:17 since the first passage mentions a drought, whereas the last one speaks of *blasting* and *mildew*, due to excessive moisture (according to André). Actually the words are of doubtful meaning "and are not referred to damp in any of the passages in which they occur, but, on the contrary, appear to be the consequences of drought." G. A. Smith adds in a footnote that these Hebrew words are used to describe the condition following drought in Amos 4:9; in other passages where they occur – Deut. 28:22; I Kings 8:37 and II Chron. 4:28 – they are mentioned in a list of possible plagues after famine, pestilence, fevers, all of which, with the doubtful exception of fevers, followed droughts.

The expression *"upon that which the ground bringeth forth"* included "all the products of the soil not previously mentioned."[69] The word *"labor"* stresses the lassitude and weariness which followed the straining of all of man's powers to the utmost. God called a waste upon all the efforts of man, especially upon the work accomplished in agriculture. The Lord had promised:

> "If ye walk in my statutes, and keep my commandments, and do them; then I will give you rain in due season, and the land shall yield her increase (Lev. 26:3, 4).

To those who feared the Lord the Psalmist had given the assurance that he would "eat the labor of his hands" (Ps. 128:2).

National disobedience brought about God's curse and all labor was vain. Our planting and watering is of no avail unless the Lord of the harvest gives the increase. Activity cannot replace obedience, nor can ritualism replace personal holiness. This lesson is strongly emphasized in the third discourse of Haggai.

---

[68]G. A. Smith, *op.cit.,* p. 229
[69]Eiselen, *op.cit.,* in loco

1:12. *"Then Zerubbabel the son of Shealtiel, and Joshua the son of Josedech, the high priest, with all the remnant of the people, obeyed the voice of the LORD their God, and the words of Haggai the prophet, as the LORD their God had sent him, and the people did fear before the LORD."*

The very first indication of a change of heart, the very purpose of obedience, is recognized by God. The resolution was carried into effect (v. 14). The expression *"the remnant of the people"* embraces all those who had returned from the exile (cf. Zech. 8:6, 11, 12). The people obeyed the voice of Haggai because (*"as"* has a causal sense here) they knew him to be God's messenger. They "received the word of God . . . not as the word of men, but as it is in truth, the word of God, which effectually worketh also in you that believe" (I Thess. 2:13).

The people *"did fear before the LORD."* They were not afraid of God, nor terrified by the supreme Ruler of the universe; they did not stand in horror before Him, nor did they dread the Almighty, for to "fear the LORD is the beginning of wisdom, and knowledge of the Holy [One] is understanding. . . . The fear of the LORD is to hate evil" (Prov. 9:10; 8:13). The word *"fear"* also implies reverence, adoration and gives adequate expression to the spirit of true religion in the Old Testament. It is the opposite of all self-assertion, of all presumptuous self-confidence (Prov. 3:7). "To this man will I look, even to him that is poor and of a contrite spirit, and trembleth at my word" (Isa. 66:2). The fear of the Lord is not exclusively an Old Testament notion. As Christians we should cultivate the "fear of the Lord" and "rejoice with trembling" (Ps. 2:11). Fear without joy is torment; joy without fear is presumption. The secret, the intimacy of the Lord is with them that fear Him (Ps. 25:14). Notice the following passages in the New Testament: Luke 1:50; 18:2, 4; Acts 10:2, 22, 35; Col. 3:22; I Peter 2:17; Rev. 14:7; 15:4; 19:5.

> "That preaching then is most warrantable, which is most profitable, and that most profitable which is most powerful, which best informs the mind, enlighteneth the judgment, affects the soul aright, and warms the heart with comforts and contentment of it."[70]
>
> "Zerubbabel the prince was needed, Joshua the priest was needed; but if the work of building the second Temple had

---

[70]Rainolds, *op.cit.*, in loco

> been left to the orders of the priests and princes, it might in all probability never have been accomplished at all."[71]

All the people of the land had to be roused to the duty and privilege of sharing in this task. The same is true regarding the spiritual temple.

1:13. *"Then spake Haggai the LORD'S messenger in the LORD'S message unto the people, saying, I am with you saith the LORD."*

Some commentators question the originality of this verse because Haggai is not called "the prophet" but rather the "*messenger.*" The expression "*Haggai the LORD'S messenger*" is not strange in the least. Prophets and priests are messengers of God (many commentators suppose that Haggai was both prophet and priest). Malachi calls the priest "the messenger of the LORD of hosts" (Mal. 2:7); John the Baptist is announced as "my messenger" (Mal. 3:1). (See also Isa. 44:26 and II Chron. 36:15.)

It is further claimed that the verse interrupts the sequence of thought, as verse 14 is the natural continuation of verse 12. Others would transpose the text after verse 14. König[72] defends the genuineness of the text and Bloomhardt writes: The sentiment of verse 13b corresponds to verse 8b and forms therefore a fitting conclusion."[73] The words are not inconsistent with the situation, since the message is given to encourage the people to proceed in the path of obedience. Neglect made the prophet "strike once and again, while the iron was hot, least the sparks which were kindled by the first sermon, should have been either quenched or cooled for want of another to second and abett the same."[74]

In Hebrew the words "messenger" and "angel" are identical, therefore "some foolish men have thought that Haggai was one of the celestial angels, clothed with the form of man"[75] (esp. some of the patristic commentators).

Haggai had a mandate from God (II Cor. 5:20) and his word of cheer was literally: "I with you." If God be for us, who can be against us. "I am" rises beyond the limits of time, "with you" beyond the limits of space. It is an all-containing

---

[71]D. Baron, *Haggai's Voice to the Present* (London), p. 7
[72]König, *Einleitung in das A.T.* (Bonn, 1893), p. 363
[73]P. F. Bloomhardt, *The Poems of Haggai,* in loco
[74]Rainolds, *op.cit.,* in loco
[75]Calvin, *op.cit.,* in loco

promise. "Who art thou . . . and who am I" (cf. Matt. 28:20 and the encouragement to erect the spiritual temple of God).

1:14. *"And the LORD stirred up the spirit of Zerubbabel the son of Shealtiel, governor of Judah, and the spirit of Joshua the son of Josedech, the high priest, and the spirit of all the remnant of the people; and they came and did the work of the LORD of hosts, their God."*

God fulfilled his promise by giving to Zerubbabel, Joshua and all the people a willingness to carry out the work. Formerly God had "raised their spirit" to return to Palestine, and now he stirred up their spirit to build the Temple. The Holy Spirit uses the word of God – used the preaching of Haggai – and applied it to the heart of man. Paul's exhortation to Timothy is to "stir up the gift of God" (II Tim. 1:6). In the wilderness "every one whose heart stirred him up, and every one whom his spirit made willing" brought offerings for the construction of the Tabernacle, so we, too, are admonished to work and build upon the foundation which is laid (Exod. 35:21).

Concerning Zerubbabel and Joshua see notes on 1:1. For the expression "remnant of the people" see 1:12.

The people *"came,"* i.e., even from the neighboring towns and from the countryside. Perhaps even those scattered in the Negeb and surrounding territories came to lend a helping hand. A preliminary work was necessary. Rubbish had to be cleared away, building material procured and prepared.

1:15. *"In the four and twentieth day of the sixth month, in the second year of Darius the king."*

Consult "Historical Background" and notes on 1:1 regarding king Darius. Exactly twenty-three days after the first message the people began to build. There was an immediate response to the prophetic message, but time was needed to gather the material and to remove the debris.

In the Vulgate this verse is the first one of Chapter 2. The impossibility of this arrangement is obvious since the dates given in our text and 2:1 do not coincide. A few commentators would like to omit this text altogether or at least eliminate the word *"sixth"* and transpose 2:15-19 after the emendated text of 1:15a and finally insert a thought similar to 2:1b, 2. According to this reconstruction the words *"in the second year of Darius the king*" become introductory to 2:1 and follow 2:19. Thus the following text is obtained:

> "On the twenty-fourth day of the month [1:15a – omit "sixth"] the word of the LORD came by the prophet Haggai to Zerubbabel the son of Shealtiel, governor of Judah, and to Joshua the son of Josedech, the high priest and to the remnant of the people [an insertion similar to 2:1b, 2]: Consider from this day . . . from this day will I bless you [the entire passage of 2:15-19, but eliminating the first words of 2:15, i.e., "and now I pray you"]. In the second year of Darius in the seventh month" (2:1 ff).

The entire transposition is based on the idea that in 2:10-14 Haggai denounces the cooperation of the Samaritans in the reconstruction of the Temple.[76] This is not accepted by most commentators and the exegesis of the passage will not allow it. The transposition and rearrangement is therefore unnecessary.

It is hardly possible that Haggai would refer to the Samaritans in 2:14, using the expression "this people" without further qualification, esp. since he uses the same designation to speak of Israel in 1:2. As in 1:5 and 7 the exhortation to "consider" in 2:15 is used transitionally, to confirm the disobedience of "this people." If 2:15-19 followed upon 1:15a, what would the expression "consider" (in 2:15) confirm? How has the transposition been effected? How and why was 2:18 added? Rothstein assumes that: both messages (1:10 and 2:10) are dated the twenty-fourth of the month (different months however!) and the redactor, overlooking the fact that different months were involved, placed the two passages in relation to each other because both were delivered on the twenty-fourth of the month. Further he neglected to change the date in 1:15a. Eissfeldt accepts this hypothesis of Rothstein.[77] He believes that the arrangement of 1:1-11 is incorrect. According to him vv. 5 to 11 gives the impression of being overloaded, verbose. He therefore questions the genuineness of some verses in this section and transposes others. He suggests that two independent collections might have confronted the redactor and he combined them into one continuous passage. According to Eissfeldt the underlying portions of these two discourses woven carelessly into one can be traced distinctly: 1:1-6, 8 and 1:7, 9-11.

Others again are of the opinion that the text is a gloss from 2:1, 10 and subsequently an editor changed the words "ninth

---

[76]Rothstein, *BWAT* (1908)

[77]O. Eissfeldt, *Einleitung in das A.T.* (Tübingen, 1934), p. 478

month" into "sixth month" to bring the text into harmony with chapter one. Several other suggestions have been made: that 1:15 originally preceeded 1:13 and introduced 2:15-19. Later 1:13 and 2:15-19 lost their primary position and somehow found their present setting, etc. There is really no compelling reason to assume transpositions, emendations or other changes. The text simply indicates how rapidly the people went to work. The verse forms a fitting conclusion to chapter one.

2:1. *"In the seventh month, in the one and twentieth day of the month, came the word of the LORD by the prophet Haggai saying,"*

The fainting courage of the people was met with a fresh message from God. The people were dispirited because they compared the edifice under construction with the splendor of the old Solomonic Temple. They needed a word of encouragement. We need and receive continuous instruction. "The good graces of God, even in the best of us, will be quickly extinguished and put out, if they be not quickened and repaired in us by by hearing the word of life."[78] The date given here corresponds with the seventh and last day of the feast of Tabernacles (Lev. 23:33). It was a festival of harvest thanksgiving (Exod. 23:16), commemorating the passage of the nation of Israel through the desert and foreshadowing the rule of God over the entire earth. This celebration, following a scanty harvest, would accentuate the contrast between the past and the present.

Great revolutions had occurred under Darius, and it had perhaps appeared that the erection of the visible kingdom was imminent, but the shaking of the nations had not issued in the glorious coming of God and the Israelites were discouraged. Small in number, economically poor because of a meager harvest — these thoughts would perhaps come to their mind on such a day and form a fitting background for the prophetic message of Haggai.

2:2. *"Speak now to Zerubbabel the son of Shealtiel, governor of Judah, and to Joshua the son of Josedech, the high priest, and to the residue of the people, saying,"*

See notes on 1:1 concerning Zerubbabel and Joshua. As to the expression *"the residue of the people"* see comments on 1:12.

The Septuagint has "and to *all* the residue" and some com-

---

[78]Rainolds, *op.cit.*, in loco

mentators would like to introduce this word into the Hebrew text (cf. 1:12, 14 and the RSV).

2:3. *"Who is left among you that saw this house in her first glory? and how do you see it now? is it not in your eyes in comparison of it as nothing?"*

About sixty-six years had elapsed since the destruction of the Temple. Some of the older men had seen Solomon's Temple in all its splendor (I Kings 6:22, 28, 30, 32; 7:48-50). How do you see it now? The real question is: How does God see it? and He declared through Zechariah: Who has despised the day of small things? (4:10).

The last clause of verse 3 may perhaps be rendered: "Is not the like of it as nothing in your eyes?' or "Is not such as it is as nothing in your eyes?"

> "It must have been in the absence of metal and carving that it (the building) was deemed so inferior to the first Temple. The holy of holies was empty. The ark, the cherubim, the tables of stone, the vase of manna, the rod of Aaron were gone. The golden shields had vanished. Even the high priest, though he had recovered his official dress, had not been able to resume the breast-plate with the oracular stones."[79]

According to Jewish tradition five things were missing in the Temple; see notes on 1:8. The ark of the covenant was not reproduced, because the "writing on the tablets had a mysterious origin." The Shekinah, the cloud of glory, was absent – in itself a proof that the restoration was as yet incomplete. The spirit of prophecy was extinct and the scribe replaced the prophet – Malachi became a lone exception. The sacred fire was missing as well as the Urim and Thummim. The Israelites

> "saw in the contrast between the new Temple and the former one, a type of the relation in which they themselves stood to God."[80]
>
> "Touching God himself, hath he any where revealed that it is his delight to dwell beggarly? And that he taketh no pleasure to be worshipped saving only in poor cottages. . . . When they, which had seen the beauty of the first Temple built by Solomon in the days of his great prosperity and peace, beheld how far it excelled the second which had not

---

[79]A. P. Stanley, *Lecture on the History of the Jewish Church* vol. III (London, 1883)

[80]Hengstenberg, *op.cit.*, 301 ff.

builders of like ability, the tears of their grieved eyes the prophet endeavored with comforts to wipe away. Whereas if the house of God were by so much the more perfect by how much the glory thereof is less, they should have done better to rejoice than weep, their prophets better to reprove than comfort."[81]

Hooker reacted against puritanical teaching. Today we may have to be reminded of the words of Minucius Felix, explaining why Christians do not worship in Temples. "What temple shall I build to Him, when this whole world fashioned by His word cannot receive Him? . . . Were it not better that He should be dedicated in our mind, consecrated in our inmost heart?"[82]

Actually reconstruction of the Temple had just begun and the comparison made is not between Solomon's Temple in its finished form and beauty and the Temple in the days of Haggai in the process of reconstruction. The comparison is more general and based on an evaluation of plans and resources. The present endeavor seemed insignificant with the ultimate achievement in the days of Solomon. Many may well have bewailed the lack of certain items of the Temple furniture. The older people who remembered the first Temple spread gloom and discouragement.

> "It is sometimes the fault of the old people, to discourage the services of the present age, by crying up too much the performances and attainments of the former age; with which should be provoked to emulation, but not exposed to contempt. 'Say not thou, that the former days were better than these' (Eccl. 7:10), but thank God that there is any good in these, bad as they are."[83]

"Who among you is left that has seen *this* house in her first glory or former glory?" (A.S.V.). In the eyes of the Israelites there was only *one* Temple. "They were all one and the same Temple of Jehovah, only in different forms."[84] Similarly the Pulpit Commentary:

> The two eras represented by these houses were not regarded as two distinct and separate periods, but as one continuous period. . . . The present was not so much a fresh commencement as a prolongation of the past."[85]

---

[81]Hooker, *Laws of Ecclesiastical Polity* vol. II, (Oxford, 1865), pp. 53 ff.
[82]*Ante-Nicene Fathers,* vol. IV (Grand Rapids, 1951) p. 193
[83]Matthew Henry in loco
[84]*The Pulpit Commentary,* vol. XIV Grand Rapids, 1950), in loco
[85]*Ibid.*

For the entire verse see Ezra 3:10 ff., where a similar feeling of despondency took possession of the people, when the foundations of the Temple were laid.

> "The people had before ceased to work, because they were immoderately devoted to their own interest, which was a proof of base ingratitude and a profane impiety . . . but the cause was different when Haggai was sent the second time; for their indifference then arose from a good principle and a genuine feeling of religion (i.e., the relative insignificance of the second Temple in comparison with the one built by Solomon). But we hence see what a subtle contriver Satan is, who not only draws us away openly from God's service, but insinuates himself in a clandestine manner, as to turn us aside under the cover of zeal, from the course of our vocation."[86]

In the first message Haggai combats the peril of false content, whereas in the second address he reacts against the peril of a false discontent. In the third discourse he warns against the peril of false expectations and closes the book with a message to dispel the peril of false fear.

We might well be discouraged when we remember the apostolic age of the church or other glorious eras in the history of the church and raise the question: How do you see it now? Yet now, be strong and work!

2:4. *"Yet now be strong, O Zerubbabel, saith the LORD; and, be strong O Joshua, the son of Josedech, the high priest, and be strong, all ye people of the land, saith the LORD, and work: For I am with you, saith the LORD of hosts."*

These words are similar to those used by David to encourage Solomon to build the first Temple.

> "Take heed now; for the LORD has chosen thee to build a house for the sanctuary: be strong and do it. And David said to Solomon his son, Be strong and of good courage and do it: fear not, nor be dismayed: for the Lord God, even my God, will be with thee; he will not fail thee, nor forsake thee, until thou hast finished all the work for the service of the house of the LORD" (I Chron. 28:10, 20).

Pusey remarks that Haggai

> "seems to have adopted the words, with the purpose of suggesting to the downhearted people, that there was need of the

[86]Calvin, *op.cit.,* in loco

like exhortation, in view of the building of the former Temple, whose relative glory so depressed them."[87] (Cf. Zech. 8:9 and 4:6.)

Be undaunted, take courage, be strong and work. These words are characteristic of Haggai and largely sum up his message. The call to duty in the first message is to build, or to be strong and work, coupled with the dynamic promise "*I am with you.*" The same holds true of the second address, where the identical thought prevails. Be strong in your innermost being and work, thereby giving expression to your determination, for "*I am with you.*"

> "Any strength that is dissociated from this assurance is not strength at all. It is mere spasmodic weakness – we cannot disconnect ourselves from the fountain of eternal strength and long remain mighty men."[88]

Finally this remark from McIlmoyle:

> "The command *be strong* is the same for all three sets of people. Their tasks may differ, but the spirit in which they are to be undertaken is the same for the prince, priest and people."[89]

Some emendations have been proposed. Omit "son of Josedech, the high priest" because it was added *honoris causa* (!). Omit also the second "saith the LORD." As a matter of fact this expression is found quite frequently in this discourse and there is no particular reason to suppress it in this instance. The style of Haggai is characterized by repetitions. Finally "ye people of the land" should apparently be replaced by "you residue of the people" as in 1:12, etc. as if the prophet was compelled to be repetitive or to use stereotyped expressions. Sometimes critics would omit certain repetitions, whereas at other times correct the text to make sure certain formulas are repeated! At times similar expressions should be deleted according to some critics, whereas others discover a different author because the vocabulary is slightly different.

2:5. "*According to the word that I covenanted with you when ye came out of Egypt, so my spirit remaineth among you: fear ye not.*"

---

[87]Pusey, *op.cit.*, in loco
[88]*Pulpit Commentary* in loco
[89]In *The New Bible Commentary* (Grand Rapids, 1953), p. 746

"The design of what the prophet says is to show that their fathers were not formerly redeemed, that their children might reject God, but that He might continue His favor to His people to the end."[90]

God confirms the promise given in the previous verse, by stating that the covenant is still in force. His Spirit is still at work in Israel, removing obstacles and hindrances. This in itself demonstrates the validity of the assertion made in verse 4 "I am with you."

Our text stands more forcibly, because abruptly. The ambiguity of the first two Hebrew words is puzzling (*et hdbr*). The first half of this verse is omitted in the Septuagint as well as by several commentators. Thus Mitchell:

"The glossator, as he read v. 4b, was evidently reminded by the words of Haggai of something similar in the history of the Exodus, and made this comment on the edge of his roll; whence it was afterward, by a copyist incorporated into the text."[91]

Actually, the first half of this verse does not break the connection. It is not necessary to supply the word "remember" (Ewald, Hengstenberg and the margin of the ASV[92]) in order to establish a connection. This is arbitrary. It is suggested that Haggai is reminding them ("remember") of the words "fear not" uttered by Moses (not God!) in an altogether different connection (Exod. 20:20). The text of Exodus 20:20 cannot possibly have such a central significance, so that the mere remembrance of this verse would infuse new courage into the hearts of the Temple builders.

Calvin[93] and the Authorized Version take *et* to be the accusative of the norm, or standard.[94]

It may be best to consider *et* to be the sign of the definite nominative of the subject. The thought then would be: "As regards the word that I covenanted with you. . . ." "The *et* is simply used to connect the new declaration with the preceding one, and to place it in subjection to the one which follows."[95]

---

[90]Calvin, *op.cit.,* in loco
[91]*Ibid.*
[92]E. W. Hengstenberg, *Christology of the Old Testament,* III (Grand Rapids, 1956) p. 237
[93]*Op.cit.,* in loco
[94]Cf. J. Ch. K. Hofmann, *Weissagung und Erfüllung,* I (Nördlingen, 1841) p. 330
[95]Keil, *op.cit.,* in loco

The "*word*" is used here to denote the Sinaitic covenant.

> Permanent validity is assured to the Word settled in Covenant form at the Exodus from Egypt, as well as permanent abode to the Divine Spirit in the midst of the Church.[96] (Cf. Exod. 19:5, 6; Deut. 7:6 and Exod. 6:7 as well as Deut. 26:17-19.)

The nation is reminded of the Sinaitic covenant which remained intact. They are still a holy nation and possess a unique relationship with God. His Spirit is still active in their midst, the Spirit of prophecy (Haggai and Zechariah), the Spirit which will conquer all obstacles (Zech. 4:6), the Spirit of God.

The word "*covenant*" is literally "to cut, to cut off," "so used from slaying and dividing the victims, as was customary in making a covenant" (Gesenius). "The two halves denote the two contracting parties, and the flame passing through denotes their union by Jehovah, who alone is He who constitutes the covenant."[97]

It is important to notice the idea of the organic unity of the nation. Haggai says: "*when ye came out.*" This thought recurs frequently in the Old Testament and is reproduced in the New Testament (Matt. 23:29 ff.).

> "The omnipotence of God can and will carry out His word, and glorify His Temple. This leads to the further promise in v. 6-9, which gives the reason for the exhortation 'Fear not.' "[98]

2:6. "*For thus saith the LORD of hosts; Yet once, it is a little while, and I will shake the heavens, and the earth, and the sea, and the dry land.*"

"*For thus saith the LORD:*" "This declaration, then, depends on the covenant before mentioned; and hence the causative particle is used."[99]

The words "*yet once, it is a little while*" have been translated differently by various commentators.

The translation adopted by the Vulgate (*ad huc unum modicum est*), "it is as yet a little while," has been followed by Luther (*es ist noch ein Kleines dahin*), Calvin, etc. This view is beset with grammatical difficulties.

---

[96]von Orelli, *Die Zwölf kleinen Propheten* (München, 1896), in loco
[97]Von Orelli, *op.cit.,* in loco
[98]Keil, *op.cit.,* in loco
[99]Calvin, *op.cit.,* in loco

–The Hebrew word translated "little" (m'ṭ) is never constructed with a feminine and yet the Hebrew word translated "once" (*'cht*) is in the feminine gender in Hebrew.

–If "once" were a numeral adjective belonging to "little" (one, or a little time), it would have to follow the substantive and could not precede "little."

Hofman,[100] Delitzsch,[101] and others render: "One period more – a brief one it is" and claim that the prophecy contains two thoughts:

–From the present time till the predicted great change of the world, will be only one period – that is, one uniform epoch – which will not be divided again into several others.

–That this period will be a short one.

However, "one" does not mean "one uninterrupted time-period."

The Authorized Version gives the best translation and is followed by the greatest number of commentators: Yet once, or one more time. "For the ellipsis of 'time' (*p'm*), where 'once' (*'cht*) stands by itself, as here, Exod. 30:10, Job 40:5, Ps. 62:12 and 89:36."[102] More references might be added to those: II Kings 6:10; Josh. 5:2; etc. It is important to notice that "yet" (*'vd*) never loses its primary sense of repetition, hence it is translated "once again" in the Revised Standard Version. This text must be studied in conjunction with the following verse:

"It is a little while."

> "The explanation which interprets this to mean 'little' in the sight of God, with whom a thousand years are as one day, is forced and unsatisfactory."[103] Indeed, "He who speaks to men, must speak according to human conceptions, or else state that he has not done so."[104]

---

[100]Hofmann, *op.cit.*, in loco

[101]Delitzsch, *Commentary on the Epistle to the Hebrews*, II (Edinburgh, 1870), p. 360

[102]Henderson, *op.cit.*, in loco

[103]Perowne, *op.cit.*, in loco

[104]Hengstenberg, *Christology of the Old Testament*, III (Grand Rapids, 1956), 238 ff.

Pusey's argument, that the time was little "in respect to the time, which had elapsed from the fall of Adam . . . little also in respect to the Christian law, which has now lasted above 1800 years" is unnatural.[105]

The text cannot have direct reference to the birth of Christ. This time-honored explanation must be set aside although maintained (esp. in the past) by many commentators. Thus for instance Augustine:

> "The fulfillment of this prophecy is in part already seen, and in part hoped for in the end. For he moved the heaven by the testimony of the angels and the stars, when Christ became incarnate. He moved the earth by the great miracle of His birth of the virgin. He moved the sea and the dry land, when Christ was proclaimed both in the isles and in the whole world. So we see all nations moved to faith; and the fulfillment of what follows, 'And the desired of all nations shall come,' is looked for at his last coming. For ere man can desire and wait for Him, they must believe and love Him."[106]

John Newton, in one of his sermons comments, that

> "the prophecy has been, in a measure literally fulfilled. At his birth a new star appeared. At his death the sun withdrew his shining, the earth quaked, the rocks rent, and the dead arose. During his life He often suspended and overruled the stated laws of nature, and exercised supreme power over the visible and invisible worlds. He shook the kingdom of darkness, spoiled principalities and powers, triumphing over them by his cross. He shook the kingdom of the earth; the idols trembled and disappeared before His gospel, till at length the Roman Empire renounced heathenism and embraced the Christian faith. . . . heaven and earth are used to denote the religious and political establishments of Israel; or, as we say, their constitution in church and state. This, without doubt, is the primary sense here."[107]

So also Pusey:

> "By the word 'yet' he looks back to the first great shaking of the moral world, when God's revelation by Moses and to His people broke upon the darkness of the pagan world, to be a monument against heathen error till Christ should come; 'once,' looks on, and conveys that God would again shake the world,

---

[105]Pusey, *op.cit.*, in loco
[106]*The City of God,* book XVIII, chap. 35
[107]John Newton, *Works,* IV (New York, 1810), pp. 29-39

but once only, under the one dispensation of the Gospel, which should endure to the end."[108]

As a matter of fact

> "the usual meaning of this symbolic act (the shaking of all things) is that of a visitation of vengeance on the enemies of God, and not an unfolding of His dispensation of mercy."[109]
>
> "Therefore will I shake the heavens, the earth shall remove out of her place, in the wrath of the LORD of hosts, and in the day of his fierce anger" (Isa. 13:13).

Haggai looked back to more than a "moral shaking." At the descent of the Lord upon Mt. Sinai – and to this event the words point according to Hebrews 12:26 – "the whole mount quaked greatly," yea, "the earth trembled," "the mountains melted before the LORD," "the earth shook," the everlasting mountains were scattered, the perpetual hills did bow (Exod. 19:18; Judg. 5:4, 5; Ps. 68:8 and Hab. 3:6). The first "shaking" which accompanied the manifestation of God to Israel was local, whereas the shaking here announced will be the precursor to the final manifestation of God and embraces all nations. The approaching shaking of the world will be more violent than the one that took place when God gave the law to Israel. The heavens and the earth, the sea and the dry ground, the nations themselves will be affected. In the letter to the Hebrews the history of the nation at the time of the exodus out of Egypt is recalled (Heb. 12:25; notice the word "they"): When God revealed Himself on Mount Sinai the earth trembled. "Tremble, thou earth, at the presence of the LORD, at the presence of the God of Jacob" (Ps. 114:7). Likewise, when God will reveal Himself through the glorious coming of Christ, all things will be shaken "once more." Haggai predicts a final shaking (*once* more), "And this word, Yet once more, signifieth the removing of those things that are shaken, as of things that are made, that those things that cannot be shaken may remain. Wherefore we receiving a kingdom which cannot be moved, let us have grace, whereby we may serve God acceptably with reverence and godly fear" (Heb. 12:27, 28).

When God shall once more shake the whole world, the conditions of the physical universe and of the world of nations shall

---

[108]*Ibid.*
[109]T. V. Moore, *op.cit.,* in loco

be totally altered. God shall "create new heavens and a new earth: and the former shall not be remembered nor come into mind" and the "new heavens and the new earth which I will make they shall remain before me, saith the LORD" (Isa. 65:17; 66:22).

> "God from the very first created that which is changeable with the purpose of establishing the continuance of that which is immutable by setting it free from the changeable elements. . . . the provisional shall be replaced by the complete, the temporal by the eternal."[110]

The final shaking shall leave behind "the world of true essential existence that cannot be shaken, the inheritance of the saints."[111] The announcement of this catastrophy is called a "promise" because it is the final triumph of God's cause – God smites and shakes in order to heal.

The shaking of the nations shall put an end to the then existing world conditions and the Lord "will overthrow the throne of the kingdoms" and "destroy the strength of the kingdom of the heathen (nations)" as Haggai himself explains our text in his last message (2:2-23).

> "The prophet looks forward from the feeble beginning of the new spiritual and national life to that final manifestation and kingdom of God in which the discipline begun on Sinai is to have an end."[112]

It follows then, that

> "the whole grand future, embracing not only the first but the second coming of Christ and the final consummation of all things, is indeed included in the prophecy. But it was the beginning of the great drama, not its last act, that was then closely at hand. The beginning was the then immediate object of the Church's hope: in that she was to welcome the promise and the presage of all that should follow."[113]

In the prophetic perspective the coming events are blended together. Prophecy blends together the beginning and the end, the preparation and the results, the commencement of redemp-

---

[110]Delitzsch, *op.cit.,* in loco

[111]A. B. Davidson, "*The Epistle to the Hebrews* (Grand Rapids, 1950), p. 250.

[112]The *Epistle to the Hebrews* by Brooke Foss Westcott (London, 1889), p. 420

[113]Perowne, *op.cit.,* in loco

tion and its consummation, our Lord's coming in humility and in majesty. All this is viewed as one continuous event, one complete whole. This is frequently illustrated throughout Scripture. Christ, speaking of the impending destruction of Jerusalem (A.D. 70), related this event to the coming of Antichrist and the final judgments in human history, because the destruction and judgment of Jerusalem was a pledge and prefiguration of the ultimate judgment and destruction of all opposing forces and enemies of God. Similarly Isaiah, after the promise of deliverance from the yoke of the Assyrian, goes over to a description of the messianic age, because the first deliverance is a type and guarantee of the final redemption (Isa. 10 and 11). The Old Testament views events "from afar" and this perspective blends near and distant events.

Haggai announces that the shaking will begin "in a little while." The explanation of Rashi is interesting:

> "After the downfall of the Persian Empire, yet one more power will subjugate you, viz. the empire of Antiochus. It will endure however a little while, and then you will behold the marvels of God with the establishment of the Maccabean rule."

Actually the prophet has in view the convulsions of the great Persian Empire whose time was soon accomplished when Alexander "shook" the Empire. Upon his death the Syrian and Egyptian Empires waged continuous war and were in turn succeeded by the Roman Empire, which, in its various forms, is the last world-empire (Dan. 2). Throughout history the shaking of the nations will continue till God breaks every power and His rule shall be established and recognized. Along with these upheavals, earthquakes shall herald the coming of the Lord. The words of Haggai have a tremendous scope and the final accomplishment shall be when "the nations of them which are saved shall walk in the light of the glory of God" (Rev. 21:24). This exposition is based on Haggai's own interpretation as given in 2:22 as well as the New Testament quotation. The text cannot have reference to the birth of Christ or to "movements in history which have disposed men to own Christ as Lord," etc. Equally unsatisfactory, but representative of liberal interpretation is the explanation offered by Mitchell, that Haggai

> "had probably not heard of the capture of Babylon and the energy Darius was displaying in a second campaign in Media.

He therefore, apparently, hoped and believed that the conflict would result in the disintegration of the Persian Empire and the complete liberation of the Jew as well as the other subject peoples."[114]

Matthew Henry comments that the "shaking of the nations" is often to the settling of the church and the establishment of things that cannot be shaken. At the final "shaking," spiritual values shall be recognized and material and perishable elements shall give place to eternal realities. The heavenly Jerusalem shall "come down from God, out of heaven" and the earth shall enter into its final rest.

2:7. "*And I will shake all nations, and the desire of all nations shall come: and I will fill this house with glory, saith the LORD of hosts.*"

This verse, even more so than verse 6, has been translated differently and consequently various interpretations have arisen.

The Authorized Version ("*the desire of all nations*") follows the text of the Vulgate ("*desideratus cunctus gentibus*"), as well as Luther ("*aller Heiden Trost*"). Henderson has: "And then the things desired by all nations shall come – and refers to the expectation of the nations to share in the blessings of the new covenant."[115]

Others have suggested: "That they [i.e., the nations] may come to the desire of all nations [i.e., the Messiah]."

The American Standard Version reads: "The precious things of all nations shall come." This agrees with the French translation of Segond (*les trésors de toutes les nations viendront*), as well as the Revised Standard Version.

The Septuagint rendered "the choice things" and Theod. of Mopsuestia, "the elect persons of all nations," the noblest, or best of them will come. Augustine combined two explanations. Commenting on 2:9 he wrote:

> "Now that this is said of the new testament, he showed a little above, where he says, evidently promising Christ 'And I will move all nations and the desired One shall come to all nations.' In this passage the Septuagint translators give another sense more suitable to the body than the Head, that is, to the Church than to Christ, have said by prophetic authority 'The Things shall come that are chosen of the Lord from all

[114]Mitchell, *op.cit.,* in loco
[115]*Op.cit.,* in loco

nations,' that is *men*, of whom Jesus saith in the Gospel, 'Many are called, but few are chosen.' For by such ones of the nations there is built, through the new testament, with living stones, a house of God far more glorious than the Temple was which was constructed by King Solomon, and rebuilt after the captivity."[116]

The reference to the "elect" is excluded not only for exegetic reasons, but also by the expression "all nations."

It is very natural that one should be reluctant to give up the direct messianic reference as given in the Authorized Version. Books have been written and sermons preached on the conscious or unconscious longing of the nations for Him who is "the Desire of all nations," i.e., Jesus Christ. Testimonies to that effect have been collected from heathen authors living before the coming of Christ. In the words of Pusey,[117] "man's heart, formed in the image of God, could not but ache to be re-formed by and for Him through an unknown God who shall reform it." However, it must be admitted that the rendering of the Authorized Version cannot be correct and that we must adopt the translation of the American Standard Version. The overwhelming majority of commentators agree with the rendering of the American Standard Version, such as Calvin, McCurdy, Hengstenberg, Adam Clarke, Keil, Moore, Vitringa, Koehler, Farrar, Eiselen, Ellicott, etc.[118] They all are opposed to the direct messianic reference. There are weighty grammatical reasons for this.

The Hebrew word translated "desire" means that which is desired, delight (Dan. 11:37; I Sam. 9:20). The word is in the singular, but collective in meaning and therefore construed with a plural. Indeed,

"the verb expressing the predicate, being in the plural masculine, while 'desire,' the subject of the preposition, is in the singular feminine, occasions no small difficulty, and presents an insuperable objection to the usual messianic interpretation."[119]

Literally the words are: "And the desire of all nations, they shall come." The reference can only be to the valuable posses-

---

116 *Op.cit.*, chap. 45; cf. 48

117 Pusey, *op.cit.*, in loco

118 Most of these commentators have been mentioned previously; the exegesis is found in loco

119 Perowne, *op.cit.*, in loco

sions of the Gentiles, their silver and gold which they will bring to the Temple and of which the prophet speaks in the immediate context (v. 8). The rendering of the American Standard Version is the only correct grammatical translation, and the verb in the plural denotes the manifoldness and variety of gifts.[120] So already Calvin:

> "The desire of all nations: This admits of two explanations. The first is that nations shall come and bring with them everything that is precious, in order to consecrate it to the service of God . . . but we may understand what he says of Christ . . . but as it immediately follows: Mine is the silver and mine is the gold, the more simple meaning is that which I first stated—that the nations would come, bringing with them all their riches."[121]

Though the messianic interpretation has antiquity in its favor and was even maintained by Rabbi Akiba (who applied it to Bar Cochba), it cannot be maintained. The subject cannot be a person since the verb is in the plural. This explains the attempt to find "the elect" in our text. The artificial exegesis of Wordsworth only demonstrates the impossibility of maintaining this position. He explains the verb as referring to the Messiah who "contains in His own single person the two distinct natures of God and Man, and the three offices of Prophet, Priest and King. Might He not be justly regarded as a collective Being."[122]

Adam Clarke admits that "this is a difficult place if understood of a person."[123] The context is definitely in favor of the translation of the American Standard Version. The shaking of the nations (not the conversion of the nations!) is no preparation of the coming of the "Desire of all ages." This shaking is not the "marvellous, supernatural, and violent impulse by which God impels His elect to betake themselves to the fold of Christ" (Calvin), but according to verse 22 the violent overthrow of the political world-system to set up God's eternal kingdom (cf. the exposition of the previous verse). The shaking mentioned in our text is not the establishment of the new gospel economy, for the shaking here must necessarily correspond to the one mentioned in 2:6 and be identical with the "shaking" mentioned

---

120*Ibid.*

121Calvin, *op.cit.*, in loco

122Chr. Wordsworth, *The Holy Bible with Notes and Introductions* (Oxford, 1877), in loco

123*Clark's Commentary* (New York), in loco

in the last discourse (2:2-23). This "shaking" cannot possibly be identified with the agitation of the mind which would be excited among the heathen by the Spirit of God after the founding of the New Covenant.

The prophetic announcement is clear. The shaking of the universe and of the nations will lead the nations to bring their most treasured possessions to the house of God.

As to the fulfillment of this prophecy, we must keep in mind the explanation of verse 6. The final "shaking" shall take place at the end of time and the ultimate result of these upheavals – namely that the nations will bring their treasures to the house of God – must also lie in the future. Parallel passages are furnished by the magnificent prophecies of Isaiah: "The abundance of the sea shall be converted to thee [i.e., Israel], the forces [or better: wealth – A.S.V.] of the Gentiles shall come to thee. . . . and I will glorify the house of my glory" (Isa. 60:5-7; cf. v. 13). The glory is manifested in the gifts of the Gentiles, which evidence their adherence to the living God (Nah. 2:9). Many commentators refer to passages such as Exodus 40:34 and I Kings 8:11 as well as Ezekiel 43:4, 5 and conclude that the glory with which the Lord shall fill this Temple is the presence of the Lord Jesus Christ during His incarnation. However, the primary and direct reference of the prophet is to the time when all nations shall come and worship God and their offerings shall be the tangible evidence of this relationship. It is true, of course, that the incarnation and redemptive death of Christ make the ultimate fulfillment of this prophecy possible. Some insist that Haggai speaks of "*THIS* house" and maintain that according to the explanation offered here, the glory did not fill *this* house. Notice however, how "*this* house" is used in verse 3 and see the comments on that text. In the eyes of God and of the Jewish nation all the Temples were but one and the same Temple, although subsisting in different forms.

On the other hand we should not overlook the historic and more immediate fulfillment. The shaking of the nations began "in a little while" (v. 6). Haggai announced the overthrow of the Persian Empire and the subsequent wars up to the time of the end. This historic "prefillment" is a pledge of an ultimate and final fulfillment. The prophecy was certainly not fulfilled by the renovation of the Temple under Herod, whose motivation was purely political. The case might be different with regard to the many offerings brought to the Temple by proselytes who, dissatisfied with the darkness of heathenism, manifested their desire to know the living God by the presentation of dedicatory offerings in the Temple. The forefathers of the Jewish nation

> "Had adorned their temple in great part with donations bestowed on them by foreigners, and had always received what had been presented to them by foreign nations . . . they had themselves placed those donations about the temple which are still visible, and had remained there so long a time."[124]

We must

> "regard the desire for the living God, awakened by the decay of heathendom and its religions, which was manifested in the adoption of Judaism by the more pious heathen, as a prelude to the fulfillment which commenced with the spread of the Gospel among the gentiles."[125]

See also II Maccabees 3:2. In connection with this last quotation from Keil we must remember that the "shaking of the nations" did not consist in their conversion, but in political upheavals and revolutions. The thought that the shaking of the nations, that wars, revolutions and similar upheavals might prepare the nations for the acknowledgment of God and lead them to offer their choicest possessions to God, is a thought of great encouragement in these troubled times. Could we reap a spiritual harvest from the devastating wars fought in the last few decades? Will people weary of war – in an attempt to obtain peace – and seek the living God? If the fifth century B.C. was marked by great political "shaking," was it not also a time of great religious fermentation and could not the same occur in our day? (See "Historical Background" and notes on 1:1.)

To encourage those who had seen the Temple of Solomon in its beauty and who were discouraged as they observed the plans and outlines of the new building, Haggai states that God will once more re-establish His gracious relationships with Israel and that the glory of the Temple shall even exceed the glory of the Solomonic Temple, because it shall be a house of prayer for all nations. In a certain sense the spreading of the gospel among the heathen (weary from oft-recurring "shakings" and

---

[124]Josephus, *Bell,Jud.* II/XVIII/3
[125]Keil, *op.cit.*, in loco

more ready to turn to God) is a partial fulfillment of Haggai's words, and especially every gift and offering received from the "heathen" for the extension of the kingdom. The promise embraces more, the ultimate development and victory of the kingdom of God, when after the last great shaking of the nations and as a result of it, the nations will bring their offerings to the new and heavenly Jerusalem, having the glory of God and "the Lord God Almighty and the Lamb are the temple of it" (Rev. 20-21). "And they shall bring the glory and honor of the nations into it" (Rev. 21:26). This is the ultimate fulfillment of the prophetic announcement of Haggai.

To summarize, Haggai comforted the Jews (2:3) with the assurance that this Temple would be glorious. The nations would be shaken. Revolutions, wars, earthquakes and convulsions, the passing away of the fashion of this world (I Cor. 7:31) would wean many from things transitory and lead them to seek eternal realities, permanent values (cf. Heb. 12). The shaking of the nations would ultimately lead them to a recognition of God and they would bring their gifts to the Temple, thereby expressing the reality of their faith. In this resides the true glory of the Temple, which was the "seat and concentration of the kingdom of God, its visible embodiment." Isolated cases of literal fulfillment occurred (cf. Josephus quoted above and the extraordinary success in the proclamation of the gospel among the heathen, dominated by lassitude from numerous "shakings"). In a sense the words are exemplified in the history of the church reaping a spiritual harvest because nations despair. However the ultimate fulfillment occurs when, after the final shaking described in Revelation 20, "the nations of them which are saved shall walk in the light of it: and the kings of the earth to bring their glory and honor to it" (Rev. 21:24).

2:8. *"The silver is mine, and the gold is mine, saith the LORD of hosts."*

The Jews may doubt that the treasures of the nations shall be brought to Jerusalem and they receive this divine reassurance. At the same time the nature of the treasures is defined – silver and gold. These gifts would be used to adorn and beautify the Temple.

> "This prophecy includes all Christian gifts and offerings to the Temple of God, material and spiritual, and will find its full accomplishment in that city of which it is written 'the kings

and the nations of the earth shall bring their honor and glory into it'."[126]

Those who hold to the direct messianic reference in verse 7 paraphrase this verse: "I am not concerned about the absence of silver and gold, for all the treasures of the earth belong to me." Silver and gold is withheld deliberately so that the attention can be focussed on the spiritual glory to come, viz, Jesus Christ.

2:9. *"The glory of this latter house shall be greater than of the former, saith the LORD of hosts: and in this place will I give peace, saith the LORD of hosts."*

It has been a matter of dispute whether one should render "*the glory of this latter house*" (A.V.), or "the latter glory of this house" (A.S.V.). Both translations are possible. The Jews did not distinguish between the first and the second house; in their eyes the different houses were but one continuous dwelling place of God (cf. 2:3, where Haggai speaks of the first (i.e., Solomonic) glory of *this* house (now under construction). Mitchell concludes that "this house, as in verse 3 means the temple, regarded as having one continuous existence, in spite of its ruined or unfinished condition."[127] To encourage the nation the prophet declares that the latter glory (in contrast to the first glory mentioned in v. 3) shall even exceed the glory the Temple possessed of old. The translation of the American Standard Version seems preferable.

As to the fulfillment of this prophecy Jewish commentators have been at great pains to explain it. Since the "second" Temple was deficient in some respects (see notes on 2:3 and 1:8) how could Haggai affirm that its glory would be greater? It has been suggested that the new Temple was more glorious because it lasted longer — but mere duration is not glory and the difference in terms of years was slight. Even if the second Temple had been more glorious in structure, this could never take the place of the cloud of glory which did not rest on the new Temple. It has even been suggested that the apostasy of the nation cancelled the divine promise.[128]

Augustine suggests that the words were fulfilled in the church, the house of God, more glorious than all material Temples, because constructed with living stones. He also admits that the

---

[126]Perowne, *op.cit.,* in loco
[127]Mitchell, *op.cit.,* in loco
[128]Megilla I/12

glory of this house, i.e., of the church is not apparent now "as it shall be when every one who is there shall be there always."[129] Those who find a direct messianic reference in the preceeding verses suppose that the glory of this Temple exceeded the glory of the previous one, because Christ was presented in the Temple. Calvin applies the text to the "excellency of those spiritual blessings which appeared when Christ was revealed, and are still conspicuous to us through faith."[130] The primary reference is certainly to actual silver and gold and other precious gifts, received to beautify the Temple. The partial accomplishment has already been considered under 2:7 (which see). The Temple will be a house of prayer for all nations – the fullness of the Gentiles will come in and dedicate their gifts to God for the furtherance of the purposes of the kingdom of God.

In this place, i.e., in Jerusalem *"I will give peace."* The word "peace" implies more than the mere cessation of hostilities. Along with earthly well-being, prosperity and welfare, the word includes the great gift of divine salvation. These blessings are based on the redeeming work of the prince of peace, who made peace through the blood of his cross (Col. 1:20). Aside from the individual application, peace will also exist among nations (cf. Isa. 2:1-5), but even when all nations are shaken, there will be peace at Jerusalem (Ps. 46).

The Septuagint has the following lengthy addition: "Even the peace of soul for a possession to every one who builds to raise the Temple."

At this particular time Zechariah delivered another address to the nation (Zech. 1:2-6).

In considering the entire passage (2:6-9) it is necessary to remember that material splendor without spiritual glory cannot be accepted by God and is worthless in His eyes. The ultimate fulfillment of these verses is not primarily material, but spiritual. To some extend the words of Haggai have been literally fulfilled in the history of the past (see exegetic notes on 2:6,7), but the greater accomplishment is certainly the final spiritual fulfillment announced on the last pages of the book of Revelation (21:22ff.). The prophecy is all-embracing, "but all this is rather implied, to be discerned by the Church in the growing light of its fulfillment, than expressed, to be understood by those to whom the prophecy was first delivered."[131]

---

[129]Augustine, *City of God,* Bk. XVIII, chap. 48
[130]Calvin, *op.cit.,* in loco
[131]Perowne, *op.cit.,* in loco

2:10. *"In the four and twentieth day of the ninth month, in the second year of Darius, came the word of the LORD by Haggai the prophet, saying,"*

The date given corresponds to parts of November and December. It was exactly three months since the first response of the people (1:14, 15). As yet there was no token of God's approval and Haggai delivers a message of encouragement. Past sacrifices seemed of no avail and the prophet deems it necessary to warn against premature expectations. We pointed out already that the first discourse cautions against a false contentment, the second message opposes a false discontentment and in this address he "now exhorts them to build from a pure motive, and not to think that they had done everything when the Temple assumed a fine appearance before the eyes of men, for God requires something else."[132]

The second year of Darius and the events of the time have been considered under 1:1 and "Historical Background." Had the news of fresh revolts within the Empire reached the people? Were they under the impression that the "shaking of the nations" which had been announced would continue and lead to the coming of the Lord? Did they think themselves immune from judgment because the ritual was performed and the Temple under construction? Another generation, smug and complacent, had aspired to see the day of the LORD, and was warned by Amos: "Woe unto you that desire the day of the LORD! to what end is it for you? The day of the LORD is darkness and not light" (5:18).

The "shaking of the nations" might revive political ambitions and dreams of freedom from the Persian yoke. The nation would be tempted to take matters into its own hand, for the evidence of the Lord's blessing had not been received in spite of the fact that the Temple was now being built. The message of Haggai addresses itself to these questions.

2:11. *"Thus saith the LORD of hosts; ask now the priest concerning the law, saying."*

The Hebrew word translated *"law,"* not having the article, is better rendered by "instruction": Ask now the priest for instruction, teaching. This instruction must, of course, be based upon the law and be derived from the law. Moses had stated that Levi shall teach Jacob God's judgments and His law to Israel

---

[132]Calvin, *op.cit.,* in loco

(Deut. 33:8-10). Malachi also declares that "the priest's lips should keep knowledge, and they should seek the law at his mouth: for he is the messenger of the LORD of hosts" (Mal. 2:7; cf. Deut. 17:8-11; 21:5; Ezek. 44:23; Jer. 18:18, "the law shall not perish from the priest"). Arbitrarily G. A. Smith contends that the answer was "based upon existing custom, but not yet committed to writing"[133]; and to the same effect Wellhausen writes that "the fountain from which flowed much of the Pentateuch was in Haggai's times still open."[134] The request is for legal advice, based upon the law of Moses, and the inferences that the law of Moses was not yet written down is quite unjustified.

2:12. *"If one bear holy flesh in the skirt of his garment, and with his skirt do touch bread, or pottage, or wine, or oil, or any meat, shall it be holy? And the priest answered and said, No."*

Suppose someone would "bear *holy flesh,*" i.e., flesh offered in sacrifice to God, and that he would carry it in the wing, or corner of the large outer garment, and touch different objects with the garment, shall the holiness of the consecrated flesh be transmitted to the garment and shall the garment transmit this holiness in turn to all these objects? Can holiness be imparted by a sacred object (the holy flesh) to another object (the garment), and be transmitted to a third object (bread, wine, etc.) by the second one (the garment)? The priest answered: No. According to the law the garment, or the skirt of the garment, would become holy through the contact with the holy flesh.

> "Speak unto Aaron and his sons, saying, This is the law of the sin-offering: In the place where the burnt-offering is killed shall the sin-offering be killed before the Lord: it is most holy. The priest that offereth it for sin shall eat it: in the holy place shall it be eaten, in the court of the tabernacle of the congregation. *Whatsoever shall touch the flesh thereof shall be holy*: and where there is sprinkled of the blood thereof upon any garment, thou shalt wash that whereon it was sprinkled in the holy place" (Lev. 6:25-27).

The garment could not hallow anything else. "Indirect contact with holiness does not make a person holy"[135] See the following verses for additional details. The idea of "holy" flesh is

---

[133]*Op.cit.*, p. 245
[134]*Op.cit.*, in loco
[135]Edgar, S., *The Minor Prophets* (London, 1962), p. 54

to be explained on the basis that "holiness is the characteristic of objects when they are separated to Yahweh."[136]

2:13. *"Then said Haggai, If one that is unclean by a dead body touch any of these, shall it be unclean? And the priest answered and said, It shall be unclean."*

Literally: "If one is unclean by a person or soul"; the word "dead" is left to be understood. The answer of the priest was formulated according to Numbers 19:22: "Whatsoever the unclean person toucheth [having become unclean by touching a corpse] shall be unclean." Death polluted, because death is the result of transgression. According to the Mosaic law the ceremonial uncleanness produced by contact with a dead body was one of the strongest (Lev. 21:10-21; Num. 11:6 ff.; 19:11-21).

The lesson is clear. Haggai approaches the subject first from the negative and then from the positive side. The two questions are:

> Can the holy make the unholy, holy?
> Can the unholy make the holy, unholy?"[137]

The first question illustrates the principle that the influence of holiness is not as far-reaching as the power of the unclean. One drop of filth will defile a vase full of water, but many drops of clean water will not purify a vase full of unclean water. Whereas a healthy man cannot communicate his health to another man by touching him, a sick man can communicate his disease. One single decayed apple thrown into a basket full of fresh apples can communicate its rottenness to the entire basket. There are many ways to vice, but only one to virtue. The power of sin is extraordinary. The fall of Adam entailed consequences for all generations.

> "Goodness can with difficulty gain a hold upon human nature, like fire upon green wood; while most men are ready and disposed to join evil, like stubble, I mean, ready for a spark and a wind, which is easily kindled and consumed from its dryness. For more quickly would anyone take part in evil with slight inducement to its full extend, than in good which is fully set before him, to a slight degree. For indeed a little wormwood most quickly imparts its bitterness to honey; while

---

[136]Jones, D. R., *Haggai,* "Torch Bible Commentaries (London, 1962), in loco

[137]Fr. C. Morgan, *Haggai, a Prophet of Correction and Comfort* (London, 1936), in loco

> not even the double quantity of honey can impart its sweetness to wormwood: and the withdrawal of a small pebble would draw headlong a whole river, though it would be difficult for the strongest dam to retain or stay its course."[138]

For additional details see commentary on the following verses.

2:14. *"Then answered Haggai and said, So is this people, and so is this nation before me, saith the LORD; and so is every work of their hands; and that which they offer there is unclean."*

> "It will be noticed that the priests and the prophets act in accordance with their functions: the former declare or interpret the precept of the law; the latter applies them."[139]

"So is this people" (cf. notes on 1:2). They are like the man who carries holy flesh in the lap of his garment and they are also like the one who has become unclean because he touched a corpse. The people argued: We are reconstructing the Temple and the ritual is restored. Why the blight on our industry? Why does God's blessing not rest upon our harvest? The prophetic answer is emphatic: The Temple is the holy sanctuary of the Lord, but the Temple does not "automatically" sanctify the entire land with its inhabitants, its products and all that the land contains. The holiness of the Temple can be communicated to the land – like the holy flesh does sanctify the garment – but whatever is raised on the ground is not necessarily holy, because holiness cannot be communicated to the third degree. Haggai could have answered that "disaster cannot always be seen as a direct consequence of folly, or sin, but it may be taken as a warning"[140], but he had a deeper insight into the problem. If experience showed that a curse was resting upon the entire economy of the nation, the reason could be found in the defilement of the nation – polluted by their neglect to build the Temple. Inasmuch as the nation is unclean, every work of their hands is polluted, even "that which they offer there," i.e., on the altar which had been rebuilt (Ezra 3:3).

Once again Haggai stresses the importance of rebuilding the Temple. When the old Temple still stood many had considered it to be "an amulet to ward off evil" and imagined that this

---

138 Gregory Nazianzen, *In Defense of His Flight to Pontus* (Grand Rapids, 1955) in "The Nicene and Post-Nicene Fathers," Second Series, vol. VII, p. 207

139 Edgar, *op.cit.*

140 *Ibid.*

house could never be destroyed and the city never be razed (Jer. 7:4). Others felt that the reconstruction of the Temple was not essential to worship and thus fell into the opposite extreme. Some believed that the Temple should be rebuilt as an expression of religious fervor and in obedience to the command of God. They had begun the work of reconstruction, but perhaps become the victims of another error. Haggai now emphasizes that holy services do not cleanse unholy persons, that good works do not compensate for the neglect of important duties. The text is a strong condemnation of ritualism, of religious rites, ceremonies and the observance of various forms of religion without corresponding inward life. Haggai contrasts inward character with outward conduct. They had gone to work and begun the work of rebuilding the house of God, but apart from a godly disposition "good" works are devoid of value. Unsanctified hearts spoil religious activity. Even the bringing of sacrifices to the altar is denounced. "Ritualism is the natural religion of the unsanctified heart."[141] The old lesson needed to be repeated, that "to obey is better than sacrifice" (I Sam. 15:22).

> "For I desire mercy and not sacrifice; and the knowledge of God more than burnt-offerings" (Hos. 6:6; cf. Amos 5:21; Micah 6:6, Ps. 24:3-6; Isa. 1:11-17; 58:3; Jer. 7:21-23).
>
> "If I regard iniquity in my heart the Lord will not hear me" (Ps. 68:18).
>
> "He that turneth his ear from the hearing of the law, even his prayer shall be an abomination" (Prov. 28:9); to the same effect Jesus in the Sermon on the Mount (Matt. 5:23, 24).

No amount of activity and "good works" can take the place of holiness. When a "bad" man engages in a "good" work, it does not purify him, but he defiles it.

> "The person who offers the service gives character to the service, and if the person is unholy and impenitent, the service is impious and insulting."[142]

As always, the application of the law by the Holy Spirit produces sin-consciousness. Even the "good" works of a believer, motivated by love to God, are imperfect and only acceptable to God through the mediation of Jesus Christ (I Peter 2:5).

---

[141]T. V. Moore, *The Prophets of the Restoration* (New York, 1856), in loco
[142]M. Dods, *Haggai* in "The Expositor," Third Series, vol. 5

What shall we say then of works not flowing from love to God, be they ever so religious, produced by unbelievers? What value toward justification could the so-called good works of unbelievers have? Works can go hand in hand with uncleanness (as in the case before us), and with a lack of love. A message addressed to a church reads: "I know thy works and thy labor. . . . Nevertheless I have somewhat against thee, because thou hast left thy first love" (Rev. 2:2, 4). Activities and gifts are not synonymous with holiness. The church in Corinth possessed many gifts but lacked love. Finally a word from Calvin:

> "Men will never receive what the prophet says here – that men not only loose all their labour, but also contract new pollutions, when they seek to pacify God by their sacrifices, unaccompanied by inward purity."[143]

Another important lesson, is that repentance – be it even national repentance – does not necessarily cancel the results of former sins. Although the guilt of sin is forgiven, the historic consequences of sin may not be removed. The consequences which in the natural order of things have resulted from our disobedience often remain. The power of the unclean is great, and the long neglect to build the Temple (which had provoked pollution) could not be outweighed by recent obedience.

It has been suggested that the author "betrays a priestly knowledge of the technicalities"[144] in 2:11 ff., and many commentators assume that Haggai was a priest.

When Haggai speaks of "*this nation*" he uses the word "*goi,*" commonly employed to describe the Gentile nations. However, the same word is frequently used to describe the Jewish nation: Zepheniah 2:9; Isaiah 1:4; etc. Nevertheless, it has been suggested that "this nation" does not refer to the Jews, but to the Samaritans, the "people of the land" (Ezra 4:4). Haggai is supposed to rebuff "unclean" applicants, ready and willing to reconstruct the Temple (Ezra 4:1-4). He declares that the santification of Israel does not render the Samaritans holy, while the pollution of the Samaritans will infect the Israelites. He therefore demands a total separation between the two nations. This theory was first proposed by Rothstein and has been accepted by Sellin, Bewer, McFayden, Elliger, etc. At

---

[143]Calvin, *op.cit.,* in loco

[144]Elliger K., *Das Buch der zwölf kleinen Prophĕten* (Göttingen, 1951), p. 37

the same time Haggai has been accused of narrow-mindedness, although he is exonerated from this accusation by Elliger[145] who otherwise espouses this theory. Although it is perfectly correct that the Samaritans had offered their help to the Jews (Ezra 4), this explanation does not fit the immediate context and the explanation given above seems preferable. The word *goi* does not justify this conclusion. On the other hand these commentators assume a break between 2:14 and 2:15 and propose several transpositions to give more weight to their theory. Several would like the following sequence: 1:15a followed by 2:15 (Rothstein), or 1:13 followed by 2:15 (Bewer) (cf. notes on 1:13 and 1:15). On the other hand several commentators feel that "attempts to restore the order of the text, particularly to move 2:15-19, are unnecessary."[146] There is no compelling reason to make the transposition. Notice that verse 15 begins with the words "and now" which could hardly follow 1:15a. Incidentally, according to Ezra 4 the conflict between the Jews and the Samaritans regarding the possible cooperation of the Samaritans in the rebuilding of the Temple took place before the activity of Haggai, namely "during all the days of Cyrus, king of Persia, even until the reign of Darius king of Persia." Israel refused the offer of cooperation without hesitation and the Samaritans made the work cease by force and power till the reign of Darius. When the Jews resumed building under the prodding of Haggai and Zechariah the offer of cooperation had been rejected long ago, and the warning of Haggai – if it concerned the Samaritans – would be anachronistic.

Because the word "prophet" is missing after the name of Haggai, Sellin[147] assumes that a redactor used the notes of Haggai to give final form to the book. Sellin assumes that the book as we have it today came into being toward 516 B.C. as a memorial book regarding the Temple.

Sellin would also omit 1:3 and 7b of Chapter 1 and place 7a, 8 after verse 11 and verse 13 after verse 15. Budde prefers to

---

[145]Elliger, *op.cit.*, p. 91 (cf. p. 85ff.). See also Sellin, *Das Zwölfprophetenbuch* Leipzig, 1922), in loco

[146]Jones, *op.cit.*, in loco

[147]Sellin, *op.cit.*, in loco. According to Sellin the word "prophet" is missing in 2:13, 14, 20. Cf. Elliger, *op.cit.*, in loco.

If the word prophet is omitted it means nothing, "for the name here occurs only in introducing his contribution to a conversation, in recording which it was natural to omit titles" (G. A. Smith, *op.cit.*, p. 230).

place 1:7, 8 after 1:4. Elliger, on the other hand, invokes metric reasons to alter the text and suggests that 1:1, 2, 12 and 14 are by the hand of a redactor, that 1:7b should be omitted (because it is copied on 1:5a), that 1:3 should follow 1:4 because it initiates a new speech and that the remaining verses are from two different sources: 1:4-6, 9-11 from one source because the admonition to build is indirect; 1:7a and 8 from another source because the exhortation to build is found *expressis verbis.* Elliger also admits that the two sections complete each other and that they are well fitted into the discourse. Similar views have already been considered in the introduction ("Authenticity") and in the notes throughout the prophecy of Haggai. Commentators who suggest such emendations, transpositions, multiplicity of authorship, glosses, etc. are far from unanimous in their views and suggestions, and there is no reason to follow these suggestions.

2:15. *"And now, I pray you, consider from this day and upward, from before a stone was laid upon a stone in the temple of the LORD."*

The American Standard Version renders correctly: "From this day and backward." The Hebrew word means exactly "upward," "to ascend"; and used here in relation to time, it means backward (Henderson, Perowne, Koehler, Ewald, Keil, G. A. Smith, et al.). Cf. our expressions "to trace the stream upward" or "down to the present time," "high antiquity." Consider the time that elapsed before you resumed the rebuilding of the Temple, before the first feeble efforts began, from this time till today. Once again Haggai admonishes his generation to "consider." "This is the characteristic, unsentimental demand of prophecy for the response of the whole man."[148] In spite of the action underway for three months (1:15) the tide of their misfortunes had not yet turned. As yet there was no prosperity. Why? Because the historic consequences of their disobedience had continued so far. The Temple had stood in the midst of Israel like a dead body, a corpse polluting the nation and rendering all unlean (2:11 ff.). For years the Temple had stood in ruins. The influence of this past neglect had a greater effect than the three months of obedience. The power of the unclean had been underscored by the prophet (see previous verses).

---

[148]Jones, *op.cit.*, p. 40

> "Repentance and new born zeal do not immediately work a change upon our material condition; but the natural consequences of sin often outweigh the influence of conversion, and though devoted to God and very industrious, we may still be punished for a sinful past."[149]

The link with the previous verses is quite obvious and the proposed transpositions (examined under 2:14) quite unnecessary.

Because a different Hebrew word is used for "temple" André supposes a different author,[150] but this has "no critical significance"[151] (cf. Zech. 6:9-15).

2:16. *"Since those days were, when one came to a heap of twenty measures, there were but ten: when one came to the pressfat for to draw out fifty vessels out of the press, there were but twenty."*

The first clause has been variously rendered: "Through all that time" (A.S.V.); "since such things were" (McCurdy); "before this was" (Keil); these different translations do not affect the exposition. To substitute: "How did you fare?" (Septuagint) is certainly arbitrary.

One came to a pile of unthreshed or unwinnowed grain and expected twenty measures, but the yield was light and gave only 50 per cent of what had been anticipated. When one came to the pressfat hoping to dip off fifty *purah,* one found but twenty. The word pressfat designates the reservoir into which the mush flowed that had been squeezed out in the press or upper vat where the grapes were trodden.

As to the Hebrew word *purah* it signifies a winepress (Isa. 63:3), but "must be used here of the vessel which was ordinarily employed to draw up the wine from the lower receptacle. It quite naturally came to be adopted as a convenient measure for such purposes."[152] It was a liquid measure of unknown quantity, perhaps, as suggested by Pusey "the ordinary quantity drawn out at one time from the press."[153] A parallel passage is found in Isaiah 5:10 where the prophet declares: Yes, ten acres of vineyard shall yield one bath, and the seed of the homer shall yield one ephah."

---

[149]G. A. Smith, *op.cit.,* in loco
[150]André, *op.cit.,* p. 27
[151]Mitchell, *op.cit.,* p. 29
[152]McCurdy, *op.cit.,* in loco
[153]Pusey, *op.cit.,* in loco

2:17. *"I smote you with blasting and with mildew and with hail in all the labors of your hands; yet ye turned not to me, saith the LORD."*

The immediate cause for the inferior quality of the crops, mentioned in the preceding verse, is given here. On *"blasting"* and *"mildew"* see notes on 1:11. Gesenius explains the first word as blasting of grain produced by the east wind, the sirocco. Similarly Calvin (in loco) and Sellin who appeals to Genesis 41:6, 23, 27.[154] For some reason Elliger assumes that the verse crept into the text as a gloss.[155] The second word refers to a yellowness, paleness, an unhealthy greenness according to Gesenius. Mitchell considers them of doubtful meaning and translates "blight and decay."[156]

> "The first word is found five times in the Old Testament in the masculine form (I Kings 8:37; II Chron. 6:28; Amos 4:9; Hag. 2:17 and Deut. 28:22); once in the feminine form (II Kings 19:26). The verb is found three times (Gen. 41:6, 23, 27). Actually the term depicts the external result without analysing the intimate cause of the disease.
>
> "The second term is found six times (four times in reference to crops, once as a sickness – Deut. 28:22 – and once to designate the change of color in the face – Jer. 30:6). The adjective occurs three times (Lev. 13:49; Ps. 68:14 and Lev. 14:37). The general reference seems to greenness, or paleness – a phenomenal description of the situation not revealing the deep underlying causes. The inference that the disease was necessarily caused by abundant moisture is unjustified and the contradiction with 1:11 only imaginary."

"Hail" is mentioned in particular because God destroyed their vines with hail (Ps. 78:47). In spite of these warnings "ye turned not to me" or, literally "yet ye not to me" or "there were none – you,"[157] i.e., none of you turned to me, no not one. The phrase is evidently modelled upon the declaration of Amos: "I have smitten you with blasting and mildew . . . yet ye have not returned unto me, saith the LORD" (4:9) – this is no reason to omit these words in Haggai as a gloss.

154Sellin, *op.cit.,* in loco
155Elliger, *op.cit.,* in loco
156Mitchell, *op.cit.,* in loco
157Pusey, *op.cit.,* in loco

2:18. *"Consider now from this day and upward, from the four and twentieth day of the ninth month, even from the day that the foundation of the LORD'S temple was laid, Consider it."*

"Now at length comes the transition indicated by 'And now' of v. 15."[158] It is "perfectly natural that the pivotal point of time should receive special emphasis,"[159] but what the precise pivotal point of time is, has been a disputed matter, mainly because of the difficulty produced by the Hebrew words translated "from" and "upward." As to the last word, it is translated "backward" in the American Standard Version. The word would then have exactly the same meaning as in verse 15. In our text however, it may signify "onward" (RSV) and be understood as pointing toward the future. The precise date is given, because – according to verse 19 – a new era is about to begin and Haggai exhorts the people to consider, to lay to heart developments from this day on. If this understanding of the text is correct, then verse 15 announces a transition and demands a look backward and verse 18 a glance forward.

Haggai seems to speak of the twenty-fourth day of the ninth month as the foundation day of the Temple (2:10, 18). This seems to conflict with Ezra 3:8-10 where a different date is furnished for the foundation of the Temple. Haggai would also be in contradiction with himself (1:15). As to the last text, it would have to be understood as giving the date when the people went to work, removed the rubbish and procured the material. See notes on 1:15. Regarding the apparent contradiction with Ezra, it may be pointed out that the work begun at that time came to a sudden end and that the date given by Ezra 4:24 corresponds with Haggai's date. "The ceremony of Ezra 3:8 was of so purely formal a character that Haggai could afford to ignore it."[160] The Temple was founded originally in 536 B.C. but the work was interrupted and the ceremony repeated when the work was resumed in 520 B.C. As a matter of fact it was in 520 B.C. that the foundation of the Temple was "really and effectively laid."[161] Eiselen suggests that the "foundations were found to be in sufficiently unsatisfactory condition to demand a relaying"[162] which is altogether possible.

---

[158]Mitchell, *op.cit.,* in loco
[159]Eiselen, *op.cit.,* in loco
[160]Driver, *Century Bible* (Edinburgh, 1906), in loco
[161]Driver, *op.cit.,* in loco
[162]Eiselen, *op.cit.,* in loco. Cf. Wellhausen and Schrader

Farrar explains that the expression "from this day" points perhaps to a time when all the arrangements had been fully made and when, at some festal gathering, stone again to be laid on stone.[163]

Those who advocate the translation "backward" interpret the text as follows: "Consider from this day, back to the day of the foundation of the Temple under Cyrus." However, the Hebrew word translated "from" (*lmn*) never has the meaning "to" (*vtsr*), and as a matter of fact the two words are frequently used antithetically: Zechariah 14:10; Micah 7:12; Judges 19:30, II Samuel 7:6 and Exodus 11:7. The Hebrew word translated "from" (*lmn*) is in no case used of the present time, but always as *terminus a quo,* the earlier time limit, distant from the present. It turns the attention of the reader from a date in the past to the future. Haggai would seem to indicate two dates: the twenty-fourth of the ninth month beginning a new era of blessings, and retrospectively, the time which had elapsed since the foundation of the Temple. Both periods are contrasted. "From the day that the foundation of the LORD'S Temple was laid" would be parenthetical and remind the Israelites of the past calamities and making the contrast with the new epoch just now beginning, even more emphatic. We could then paraphrase: "Consider now from this day, the twenty-fourth of the ninth month and onward and contrast it with the time elapsed before, since the foundation of the Temple was laid." This rendering would explain the twofold "consider," since Haggai resumes his thought, interrupted by a parenthesis.

Some expositors simplify the problem by declaring 18b spurious and retain only: "Consider now from this day and upward." This is necessary when the verse is transposed after 1:15a. Regarding this see "Authenticity" and notes under 2:14.

Whether the meaning "onward" or "backward" is preferred, Haggai is not in contradiction with himself (1:15), nor with the account in the book of Ezra (3:10). Zechariah indicates that on the twenty-fourth day of the eleventh month the rebuilding had not yet advanced very far (Zech. 1:16; 4:9 and 8:9). It has also been suggested that Jeremiah 41:4-5 indicates that the stone foundation was laid at that time; actually the expression "the house of the LORD" merely indicates that these men came to the place on which the Temple had stood.

---

[163]Farrar, *Minor Prophets* (London), in loco

2:19. *"Is the seed yet in the barn? yea, as yet the vine, and the fig tree, and the pomegranate, and the olive tree, hath not brought forth: from this day will I bless you."*

A negative answer is expected: No, the seed, i.e., what the sowing yields, the corn (as in Lev. 27:30) is no longer in the barn. It has been consumed and used up in sowing. Haggai gave this address the ninth month, corresponding to part of November and December. No immediate change could be expected. The very fact that they had been able to sow was a small indication of God's favor, as perhaps in times past the prolonged drought made even sowing impossible. Haggai enumerates the principal harvests and the essential economy of the nation which depended on the vine, the fig, the olive, etc. The fruit trees had not yielded much in the past and up to the present. As yet none could predict the outcome of next year's harvest. Haggai gives the divine assurance: *"I will bless you."* The people wondered why the divine favor had not yet returned in spite of the fact the rebuilding of the Temple had been resumed. Haggai had pointed out that the power of the unclean has lasting effects and that even the ritual was "unclean" in God's eyes if devoid of the right disposition of the heart. Since three months the work had been resumed and as yet they possessed no evidence of divine blessing, token of the divine forgiveness. The prophet encourages them to trust God's promise: *"From this day will I bless you."* This, in short, is Haggai's answer to the false expectation of the nation. Every discourse of the prophet is marked by an extraordinary promise.

In connection with the word *"barn"* attention has been called to a description given by Albright of a grain-pit. One is more fully described as being oval in shape, 475 x 360 cm with an average height of 170 cm. Access was obtained through a roughly arched doorway on the north, with a flight of steps leading up and out. In the roof were three round holes, each 45-50 cm in diameter, and covered by large stones. The pit was built under Roman domination, toward the time of Christ. Grain was certainly not always stored in pits (cf. Jer. 41:8), or in dry cisterns hewn out of the rock.

2:20. *"And again the word of the LORD came unto Haggai in the four and twentieth day of the month, saying,*

This message was delivered on the same day as the preceding one. It stresses God's care over the ruler of the nation in the midst of international upheavals. Throughout the "shaking of the nations" God's kingdom shall remain unmoveable.

As to the critical views of Böhme regarding these last few verses, see "Authenticity."

2:21. *"Speak to Zerubbabel, governor of Judah, saying, I will shake the heavens and the earth."*

This message stands in direct relation to a previous address (2:6-9) and indicates when the fulfillment of these promises is to be expected. It is incorrect to assume that these verses refer only to the result caused by the "revolts of races and provinces, which threatened to disrupt the Persian empire upon the accession of Darius in 521."[164] The general collapse of the empire did not take place at that time since Darius was able to quench the revolts. Besides this message was delivered in 520 B.C. when order had largely been restored throughout the empire. If — as several critical commentators assume — the prophecies of Haggai were put in final form by a redactor living a few (or many?) years after Haggai, then the reference to the tumults under the early rule of Darius is even more impossible. Yet, the same commentators hold both views which can hardly be reconciled. It is assumed by these exegetes that Haggai's dream was not fulfilled, that Israel did not become independent under the leadership of Zerubbabel and that the prophet had to lament "his unfulfilled hope in Zerubbabel."[165] Similarly Bewer: "Haggai had proclaimed again the messianic hope, but it was nationalistic and purely political and never fulfilled."[166] It has even been assumed that Zerubbabel was raised to the throne of Judah (Sellin appeals to Zech. 6:9-15[167]) to establish the messianic kingdom but that this attempt failed and that he was presumably killed by the Persians who meted out this type of punishment to all rebels. Sellin refers to Psalm 89:39-52 in this connection,[168] but also recognizes that Zerubbabel may have survived this abortive attempt since descendents of Zerubbabel are mentioned in the genealogies of Chronicles. This reconstruction of history is highly fantastic since really nothing is known re-

---

[164]G. A. Smith, *op.cit.*, in loco

[165]*Ibid.*

[166]Bewer, J. A., *The Literature of the Old Testament* (New York, 1947)

[167]Sellin, E., "Serubbabel" in *Realencylopädie für Protestant Theologic und Kirche*

[168]*Ibid.*

garding Zerubbabel subsequent to the reconstruction of the Temple and no particular inference should be drawn from the silence. Elliger also assumes that Zerubbabel was considered the messiah of the new community[169] but this view does not even do justice to the text. It is not the overthrow of the Persian Empire which is predicted here, but a universal one; not only one heathen kingdom shall be shaken but, "The kingdoms of the heathen"; as Pusey remarks correctly, "not a change of dynasty, but a destruction of their strength," is announced. When Darius acceded to the throne revolts raged throughout the empire, but it was not assailed by a foreign enemy. The shaking of the heavens and the earth did not take place at that time, nor in 520 B.C. when this prophecy was uttered. It will occur later according to 2:6-9 and the exposition found in Hebrews 12. The prophets should not be down-graded to the role of political adventurers. They proclaimed the message of God and Haggai is announcing the reversal of human values and not preaching political agitation (cf. notes on 2:9 ff.).

A word should be added here regarding the identification of Zerubbabel with Sheshbazzar (cf. notes on 1:1). The name Sheshbazzar, from Shamash-apal-usur or Shamash-bel-usur, means "O sun-god, protect the son" (or "the lord"). If it is maintained that Sheshbazzar is to be identified with Shenazar (I Chron. 3:18) then the original might well have been "sin-ab-usur," i.e., moon-god, protect the father (see notes under 1:1). If this identification is accepted, then Zerubbabel would be a nephew of Sheshbazzar, and the latter be approximately 60 years old in 539 B.C. and certainly yield to his nephew by 520 B.C. It has also been observed that Jehoiachin was only 18 years old when the Babylonians captured Jerusalem and the king went into captivity. No mention is made of any children at that point, i.e., according to II Kings 24:8, 12 and 15. Jehoiachin remained in prison for 37 years (II Kings 25:27) from about 597 B.C. to 560 B.C. (or 561 B.C.). If Zerubbabel was the grandson of Jehoiachin he could not be the leader of the Jewish exiles in 537 (or 538) B.C.! It has been suggested that this makes the identification of Sheshbazzar with Zerubbabel very questionable. This argument would be conclusive if the relationship between Jehoiachin and Zerubbabel were not so obscure (see notes on 1:1). Finally,

---

[169]Elliger, *op.cit.*, in loco

> "in recently published tablets from a royal archive of Nebuchadnezzar, dating in and about the year 592 B.C., Jehoiachin and five of his sons, as well as at least five other Jews, are mentioned among the recipients of rations from the royal court. It is significant that Jehoiachin was still called 'king of Judah' in official Babylonian documents."[170]

If Jehoiachin had five sons in 592 B.C. a grandson could well be the leader of the returning exiles in 538 B.C. This archaeological discovery would also rule out the theory that Shealtiel was adopted by Jehoiachin (? suggested under 1:1, unless the adopted sons are the very ones mentioned in the inscription!). The identification of Sheshbazzar with Zerubbabel has been maintained by many commentators and remains possible. Those who find two different persons here (presumably uncle and nephew) suggest that Sheshbazzar passed the baton to Zerubbabel or that the former was the official head of the Jews and the latter the moving spirit in the rebuilding of the Temple. Further archaeological discoveries may help elucidate the enigma. At any rate we have no reason whatsoever to assume that Zerubbabel rebelled against the Persian overlord and that Haggai encouraged these political ambitions by his prophetic message. As to the exposition see the following verses and notes on 2:6 ff.

The Septuagint adds "and the sea and the dry land" in imitation of 2:6.

2:22. *"And I will overthrow the throne of the kingdoms, and I will destroy the strength of the kingdoms of the heathen; and I will overthrow the chariots and those that ride them; and the horses and their riders shall come down, every one by the sword of his brother."*

The word "throne" is in the singular and either used collectively or distributively, i.e., every throne of every kingdom. The word "throne" stands for rule or government as so often in Scripture. These versese are parallel to Ezekiel 38:19-21: "Surely, in that day there shall be a great shaking in the land of Israel. . . . all the men that are upon the face of the earth, shall shake at my presence. . . . every man's sword shall be against his brother."

---

[170]W. F. Albright, *The Biblical Period from Abraham to Ezra* (New York, 1963), p. 85

Zechariah confirms the word of his contemporary by declaring:

> "And it shall come to pass in that day, that a great tumult from the LORD shall be among them; and they shall lay hold every one on the hand of his neighbor, and his hand shall rise up against the hand of his neighbor" (14:13 and cf. Judg. 7:22).

Self-destructive and mutually destructive wars shall rage on the earth and the power of the heathen shall be overthrown — by God. Nation shall rise against nation, the powers of heaven shall be shaken and then shall appear the sign of the Son of man in heaven (Matt. 24:7, 29, 30). "And in the days of these kings shall the God of heaven set up a kingdom, which shall never be destroyed" (Dan. 2:44; cf. Rev. 19:11-21 and Dan. 7:21). Then the chariot shall be cut off and "I will cut off the horses, and I will destroy the chariots" and the Prince of peace shall rule the world (Ps. 20:7). Since the reference to 2:6-9 is unmistakable, it is obvious that the final accomplishment must coincide with the one indicated in the second message of the prophet. Therefore the ultimate fulfillment of Haggai's inspired word will take place after the last great revolt (Rev. 20:7-10), introducing the new heavens and the new earth (see notes on 2:6-9.)

2:23. *"In that day, saith the LORD of hosts, will I take thee, O Zerubbabel, my servant, the son of Shealtiel, saith the LORD, and I will make thee as a signet: for I have chosen thee, saith the LORD of hosts."*

Once more we must set aside shallow liberal interpretation. Haggai did not forget the inspiring ideas of the "second" Isaiah, nor that Israel as a nation had now inherited the promises made to David (?), and become the servant *par excellence* to carry the salvation of God to the ends of the earth. Haggai did not "revive" the doctrine of an ideal king, nor identify Zerubbabel with the long-expected son of David. The messianic promise, centered in a person — and fulfilled in Christ — was never transferred to the nation as a whole and had never been forgotten to the point where the messianic hope needed to be "recreated." That Haggai, carried away with a messianic concept and misreading the signs of the times, identified Zerubbabel with the Messiah is another gratuitous assumption. It has even been suggested that Psalm 21 glorifies the coronation of Zerubbabel. Other passages, such as Isaiah 9:5, 6 and 11:1-6; Micah 5:1, 3 and Psalm 110 are also applied to Zerubbabel. "Possibly Zerubbabel was crowned in secrecy."[171] but although "the star of prophetic hope" he was "quenched in darkness."[172] Actually "the nations did not press into the Second Temple of the prophet, here anticipated; the kingdoms of the world were not overthrown, the messianic age did not at once begin, and the governor Zerubbabel held no honourable place in it . . . ideals which, in the sense in which they were spoken, of, remained unfulfilled."[173] Prophecy is degraded into mere astute human insight and calculation, the observation and evaluation of political events, the outcome of which was "predicted" in the name of God and, of course, more than once erroneously. The authority of the word of God is destroyed, its inspiration denied and history "reconstructed."

There is no doubt, says Calvin, but that the prophet "points out Christ in the person of Zerubbabel."[174] Even the Rabbis recognized the messianic element of this prophecy.[175] The "representative use of this Davidite" can be compared with the one made of Joshua by Zechariah (Zech. 3). Riehm views the passage "according to the analogy of Gen. 12:3 cf. with Gen. 18:18, 22:18" and believes that it "is to be understood not merely of the person of Zerubbabel, but of him and his family."[176] The personal address to Zerubbabel is justified by the fact that he was the representative of the royal house of David, one of the ancestors of the Messiah.[177] The word "my servant" may well be an allusion to the well-known usage of the term in Isaiah. The entire sentence is solemn and certainty is indicated by the repetition of the expression "LORD of hosts" and "saith the LORD" in the very center of the text. On the expression itself see 1:7.

---

[171]Calkins, *op.cit.,* in loco

[172]Matthews, *Exposition of Haggai,* in American Commentary on the Old Testament, in loco

[173]Driver, *op.cit.,* in loco. Similar quotations could be multiplied from various liberal commentators.

[174]*Op.cit.,* in loco

[175]Hirsch, *Die zwölf kleinen Propheten* (Frankfurt, 1900), in loco; similarly Abarbanel.

[176]*Messianic Prophecy,* in loco. Similarly Bleek in his *Einleitung in das A.T.,* sixth edition, prepared by Wellhausen (Berlin, 1893) p. 380

[177]Wieseler asumes that the genealogies in Matt. and Luke represent the two lines of David's descendents via Solomon and Nathan and that the Zerubbabels mentioned there are two different persons with the same name (Studien und Kritieken, 1845), p. 397 ff.

"I will make thee a signet." This thought is echoed in the book of Sirach: How shall we magnify Zerubbabel? – He indeed was a signet on the right hand (Sirach 49:11). Great importance was attached to the signet ring. When a king gave his seal to a man he thereby elevated him to great dignity (Gen. 41:42; cf. I Macc. 6:15). The sentence announced to Jehoiachin ("though Coniah the son of Jehoiachin king of Judah were a signet upon my right hand, yet would I pluck thee hence – Jer. 22:24) is reversed and the messianic promise made to David, transferred to the line of Zerubbabel and his family among the descendents of David. "There will I make the horn of David to bud: I have ordained a lamp for mine anointed" (Ps. 132:17). The burning lamp is a natural metaphor for the preservation of the dynasty of David. Thus "in a theocratic relation Zerubbabel was the restorer of the dynasty of David."[178] Similarly Orelli: The Anointed of the Lord towers in personal individuality above the nation, exhibiting to view the nation's intimate union with God."[179] The words point to the future and are given to Zerubbabel only in so far as he was the civilian ruler of the people and represented the house of David. He is a type of Christ, the true servant of God and God's signet ring. All that has validity in God's eyes, bearing the seal, the stamp of His approval, comes to us through Jesus Christ. He is the "confirming sign of everything divine made known to the world, for God's initial is engraven on Him in unique fashion."[180] Christ seals God's purposes and is clothed with His authority. It is in Christ that we find the fulfillment of this promise. If, at the time, the kingdom of God appeared humiliated and powerless, it will nevertheless never be extinct because God is faithful to His promises. When all the kingdoms of the earth shall be shaken, God's care – symbolized by the signet-ring – will forever continue for His own. Through the line of Zerubbabel will come the Messiah, expectation of Israel. In that day when all earthly kingdoms fall, the kingdom of God shall remain and endure for ever (Luke 1:32, 33).

Zerubbabel was a type of Christ. He led Israel out of the Babylonian exile and Christ delivered from the bondage of sin; Zerubbabel built the temple of God and Christ is building the spiritual temple, the church. Christ is the signet ring in and

---

[178]McCurdy, *op.cit.*, in loco
[179]Orelli, *op.cit.*, in loco
[180]*Ibid.*

through whom all divine purposes are sealed.[181] After the final shaking of the nations we shall receive a kingdom that cannot be moved and all nations shall walk in the light of God and He shall be all in all.

> "Seeing then that all these things shall be dissolved, what manner of persons ought ye to be in all holy conversation and godliness, looking forward and hasting unto [or earnestly desiring] the coming of the day of God, wherein the heavens being on fire shall be dissolved, and the elements shall melt with fervent heat?" (II Peter 3:11, 12).

In the expectation of this great and glorious day may we gain encouragement from the message of Haggai to build the spiritual Temple of the Lord, strong in His promise and willing to hear the call "be strong and work."

---

[181]Regarding the signet ring or seal consult Bible dictionaries which furnish abundant information both Biblical and archeological.

BIBLIOGRAPHY

André, T., *Le Prophète Aggée* (Paris, 1895).

Baron, David, *Haggai's Voice to the Present Time*
Bewer, J. A., *The Literature of the Old Testament* (New York, 1947)
Bloomhardt, P. F., "The Poems of Haggai," *Hebrew Union College Annual,* vol. 5, 1928
Böhme, *Zeitschrift für alttestamentliche Wissenschaft* (ZAW) (Giessen, 1887) Zu Maleachi and Haggai.
Bright, J., *A History of Israel* (Phil., 1958) pp. 341-355

Calkins, R., *The Modern Message of the Minor Prophets* (New York, 1947)
Calvin, John, *Commentaries on the Twelve Minor Prophets,* vol. 4 (Grand Rapids, 1950)
Cashdan, *The Twelve Prophets,* "Soncino Books of the Bible" (Soncino Press, 1948)
Cornill, C. H., *The Prophets of Israel* (Chicago, 1917)
Creelman, H., *An Introduction to the Old Testament* (New York, 1917)

Dächsel, *Dächsel's Bibelwerk,* vol. 4 (Leipzig)
De Vaux, *Revue Biblique,* 1937
Dods, Marcus, ed., *Handbook for Bible Classes* (Edinburgh, 1881)
———————, "Haggai," *The Expositor,* Third Series, vol. 5
Driver, S. R., *Minor Prophets,* "The Century Bible" (Edinburgh, 1906)
———————, *Introduction to the Literature of the Old Testament* (New York, 1910)

Edgar, S., *The Minor Prophets* (London, 1962)
Eiselen, F. C., *The Minor Prophets* (New York,1907)
Eissfeldt, O., *Einleitung in das A.T.* (Tübingen, 1934)
Elliger, K., *Das Buch der zwölf kleinen Propheten* (Göttingen, 1951)

Farrar, F. W., *The Lives and Times of the Minor Prophets* (James Nisbet and Co., London)
Frey, H., *Das Buch der Kirche in der Weltwende* (Stuttgart, 1957)

Henderson, E., *Commentary on the Minor Prophets* (Andover, 1868)
Hengstenberg, E. W., *Christology of the Old Testament* (Grand Rapids, 1956)
Henry, Matthew, *Matthew Henry's Commentary on the whole Bible.*
Hirsch, M., *Die zwölf kleinen Propheten* (Frankfurt, 1900)
Hitzig, F., *Die zwölf kleinen Propheten* (Leipzig, 1841)

Hoonacker, *Les douze petits prophètes* (Paris)
Horst, F., "Die zwölf kleinen Propheten," Th. H. Robinson and F. Horst (Tübingen, 1954) in *Handbuch zum A.T.*

Jones, D. R., *Haggai*, "Torch Bible Commentaries" (London, 1962)

Keil, C. F., *Commentary on the Minor Prophets* (Edinburgh, 1892)
Kirkpatrick, A. F., *The Doctrine of the Prophets* (London, 1909)
Kittel, G., "Haggai" in *Realencyklopädie für Protestant Theologie und Kirche*
Koehler, A., *Die nachexilischen Propheten* (Erlangen, 1860)

Marti, *Das Dodekapropheton* (Tübingen, 1904)
Matthews, I. G., *Exposition of Haggai* in "An American Commentary on the Old Testament" (Philadelphia)
McCurdy, J. F., *Exposition of Haggai* in "Lange's Commentary" (New York, 1902)
McIlmoyle, J., *Exposition of Haggai* in "The New Bible Commentary" (Grand Rapids, 1953)
Mitchell, H. G., *Exposition of Haggai* in "International Critical Commentary" (Edinburgh, 1912)
Moore, T. V., *The Prophets of the Restoration* (New York, 1856)
Morgan, Fr. C., *Haggai, A Prophet of Correction and Comfort* (London, 1936)

Newton, B. W., *Israel in the days of Haggai and Zechariah with a note upon the prophecy of Haggai* (London, 1911)
Noth, M., *The History of Israel* (New York, 1960) pp. 289-316
Nötscher, F., *Zwölfprophetenbuch* (Würzburg, 1948)
Nowack, D. W., *Handkommentar zum A.T.* (Göttingen, 1922)

Olmstead, A. T., *History of the Persian Empire* (Chicago, 1948)

Perowne, T. T., *Exposition of Haggai* in "Cambridge Bible for Schools and Colleges" (Cambridge, 1908)
Pusey, E. B., *The Minor Prophets* (London, 1878)

Rainolds, John, The prophecy of Haggai, interpreted and applied in Sunday Sermons (Edinburgh, 1864)
Richter, H., *Erklärte Hausbibel* (Barmen, 1837)

Schrader, E., *Die Dauer des zweiten Tempelbaues* in "Theolische Studien und Kritieken" (Gotha, 1867)
Schumpp, P. M., *Das Buch der zwölf Propheten* in "Herder's Bibelkommentar" (Freiburg, 1950)
Sellin, E., *Das Zwölfprophetenbuch* (Leipzig, 1922)
Smith, G. A., *The Book of the Twelve Prophets* in "Expositor's Bible" (New York, 1898)
Steinmann, J., *Le Livre de la Consolation d'Israël* (Paris, 1960)

Theiner, J. A., *Die Heilige Schrift des A.T.* (Fünfter Theil) (Leipzig, 1828) von Orelli, C., *Die zwölf kleinen Propheten* (München, 1896)

Wolff, H. W., *Haggai* in "Biblische Studien" (Gieszen, 1951)
Wordworth, Chr., *Commentary on the Holy Bible* (London, 1877)

Young, E. J., *An Introduction to the Old Testament* (Grand Rapids, 1950)

Throughout the commentary reference is made to other books, not listed in the biblography and it is self-evident that many other relevant books have been consulted, such as Bible dictionaries, sermons, commentaries, books on archeology, etc.